Sex is the origin of all religions, and tantra is the art of spiritualising sexuality.

Tantra is not a religious philosophy yet it embraces a deep spiritual understanding of life. It is an ancient art of living in harmony with yourself, and with others. It offers practical tools of letting go all emotional and cultural conditioning.

Tantra is total surrender to what is, so that universal energy can again flow through us like a river without effort.

Tantra is the ultimate yoga — the Sanskrit word for unity. It unites bodies, minds, hearts and souls. It is about becoming whole and total.

This book shows the path of spiritual growth, spiritual understanding and progress while living in this real world of relationships, career and responsibility.

The Author

VIKAS MALKANI is one of the world's leading teachers of spiritual awakening, personal growth and self-awareness. Over the years he has been called a spiritual guru, zen master, soul-coach, master motivator and mystic.

Originally from India, he is the founder of SoulCentre, a holistic school based in Singapore that is dedicated to awakening the human spirit in each individual.

He is also an internationally best selling author and a keynote speaker who addresses conferences and events worldwide.

His forte is to make the ancient wisdom simple to understand and easy to apply, to create a life of health, harmony and abundance on all levels. He guides students from all over the world on the path to self-realization.

He seamlessly blends inner awareness with outer prosperity. Those who know him closely say he symbolizes the harmony of yin and yang.

Vikas is a disciple of Swami Rama of the Himalayas and has been trained in the wisdom lineage of the Himalayan Masters that involves the disciplines of meditation, spiritual wisdom and yoga.

Tantra Demystified

Tantric Secrets and Techniques for Sexual and Spiritual Bliss

Vikas Malkani

Orient Paperbacks

DELHI | MUMBAI | HYDERABAD

Dedication

To Sally, the Shakti in my life —
With your energy merged into mine, the circle is complete!
Thank you.

Acknowledgements

To the many teachers, known and unknown, who have taught me about the art of living an authentic life through their words and their silence, their actions and their inactions, their questions and their answers. This work is dedicated to you.

www.orientpapberbacks.com

ISBN 13: 978-81-222-0478-0
ISBN 10: 81-222-0478-3

1st Published in Orient Paperbacks 2009

Tantra Demystified

Published in arrangement with
Juhn Hunt Publishing Ltd., UK

Published by
Orient Paperbacks
(A division of Vision Books Pvt. Ltd.)
5A/8, Ansari Road, New Delhi-110 002)

Printed in India at
Saurabh Printers Pvt. Ltd., Noida

Cover Printed at
Ravindra Printing Press, Delhi-110 006

Contents

'Sexuality; Never repress it!

Never beg against it, rather go deep into it with great clarity, with great love. Go like an explorer. Search all the nooks and corners of your sexuality and you will be surprised and enriched and benefited. Knowing your sexuality, one day you will stumble upon your spirituality. Then you will become free. The future will have a totally different vision of sex. It will be more fun, more joy, more friendship, and more a play than a serious affair as it has been in the past. Sex is just the beginning, not the end. But if you miss the beginning, you will miss the end also.'

Osho

A Word About The Language

I have tried to avoid using too many terms from Eastern lovemaking traditions as some people may find them awkward and foreign to use or may think the words have spiritual or religious overtones.

However, I have borrowed a few terms from Tantric writings from ancient India because they suit my approach to lovemaking by adding some romantic language and special-ness. For the word penis I use '*lingam*', which means 'wand of light, pillar of life'.

For vagina I use the Indian word '*yoni*', which means 'sacred place, field of pleasure'.

Vikas Malkani

Introduction

Sex is the Origin of All Religions! Please don't be shocked with this declaration. Hear me out.

Many of us have experienced religious and cultural conditioning since our childhood that has suppressed the entire ground of sexuality. Instead of seeing the sacred in sex, it has only conditioned us to glimpse the play of temptation in it.

However if you look honestly at the sexual energy that you feel so freely within you, and where it naturally takes you in its expression, you will arrive at a simple conclusion. The first experience that man had of total stillness of mind, of pure one-pointed-ness, of bliss and ecstatic rapture, occurred in the climax of lovemaking.

Man first glimpsed God in the climax of orgasm. That's when he experienced and understood what it means to be timeless, one-pointed, without thought, and total. That's when man first lost his own boundaries and merged into something larger than himself. That's when man, a mortal, first tasted immortality. That's when man became aware of Divinity, of God.

From that one burning desire to understand and recreate that experience of one-ness, all the religions and philosophies of this world as we know them today have originated. Making love was the first experience where we lost our small self to a larger whole, and we try to recreate this experience through the religions we follow.

Unfortunately, along the thousands of years that have passed during which man has misinterpreted the teachings of ancient masters, most religious philosophies barring a few, have become very sex-negative. They feel more comfortable condemning sexuality rather than in understanding it. To befriend it and use it for their own emancipation is a far cry. By doing so, they have divided man against himself and created vast chasms in the bond that should exist between man and woman in the physical and emotional planes.

The sexual energy within us is simply a part and an expression of our very life force, the energy that keeps us alive and creative. In fighting with his sexuality, or in denying it, man fights with his own life force. He denies himself. In his journey to wholeness, he becomes his own biggest enemy when he denies the sexual aspect of his self rather than trying to understand it and use it.

Only two disciplines over the years have stood the test of time and have continued to develop deeper and deeper insights into the nature of our sexual energy. They have studied how to make sexuality a means of spiritual growth, expansion of awareness and the creation of health and harmony, within and without. These have been the disciplines of Tantra and the Tao.

Tantra is a spiritual discipline that came into being based on the life experiences of the earliest observers of life around 5,000 to 10,000 years ago. Even though today Tantra is thought to be a part of the yoga tradition, I believe that Tantra pre-dates yoga as a system to one's own divinity and enlightenment. Man was making love long before he was studying the animals around him from which the practice of yoga arose as the world knows it today.

Tantra was designed to lead the practitioner to wholeness, and was about all aspects of life, not just the sexual one. Sex was simply another means to spiritual awareness for the Tantric master. Sexuality could be used to see the divinity within, in yourself and in your partner. Tantra accepts the fact that we are all essentially sexual beings because we come to this life through the very act of sex. Sexual energy and its expressions will always be a part of our life expression from the larger perspective. Tantra accepts the whole and uses the whole.

Tantra is not simply about the physical act of sex, It understands that sex begins in the mind far earlier than in the body. Tantra is about the understanding of the mind, and its nature and expressions, one of which happens through the act of making love to another.

Tantra is about the understanding yourself and another, about healing and completing, about harmony and freedom.

The Tao, which came into being in China, is thought to be around 3,000 years old now and carries many of the concepts taken from the teachings of the tantric masters.

What is Tantra?

> *'Tantra is where sex is transformed into love and love is transformed into the higher self.'*
>
> Osho

Tantra is a Sanskrit word that has various meanings, one of which can be translated to mean 'weaving'.

Tantra is a spiritual belief system that originated in ancient Hindu and later, the Buddhist cultures of India and Tibet, which views the material world as a manifestation of the Divine. In Tantra, everything is accepted and connected — woven together.

The apparent division between body and spirit, between matter and energy, is an illusion. By consciously uniting perceived opposites (male and female, light and dark, good and bad) human beings can transcend dualism and know that all is one.

The schools of Tantra employ various forms of meditation, sacred sound, breath control, secret practices, and prayerful thought as aids to enlightenment. Many schools of Tantra incorporate sexual activity as a means of spiritual awakening. The union of an ordinary woman and man becomes the mystical coupling of a god and goddess, Shakti (Divine Energy) and Shiva (Immortal Spirit).

When connected in sacred, conscious sex, our human bodies — mirrors of the cosmos — rejoin the wholeness of essential reality. Tantra weaves together sex and spirit.

This is how I have used the term Tantra in my work and in the title of this book: as an integration of sex and spiritual growth.

British scholars and travellers returning from India first introduced Tantra to the West in the middle of the 19th century. Foremost among them was Sir Richard F. Burton (1821-1890), co-founder of the Kama Shastra Society, through which he privately published his translation of the Eastern texts, *The Kama Sutra, 1,001 Arabian Nights,* and *The Perfumed Garden.*

Tantra originated in India and later moved to Tibet and Nepal, but other cultures, such as the Taoists in China also gradually developed sacred sex traditions that encouraged the intentional cultivation of sexual energy for spiritual growth, longevity, and creativity, as well as enhanced pleasure.

Tantra philosophy can be summarized with the following four simple principles.

4 Tantra Principles

1. Sex is good and wholesome. This includes physical pleasure and considers sex as a positive force. Sex, in balance and enjoyed consciously, is good because it is what people who love each other naturally do. It is normal and healthy human behaviour.

Consensual sex between adults is a primary expression of love. Among our most basic biological needs, sex is essential for reproduction and the survival of the race. Beyond this, it is also a primary way to fulfil healthy human desires for physical touching, deep pleasure, and emotional intimacy.

2. Sexual energy and spiritual energy are the same energy. Both energies are examples of 'life force energy'. There are no words for this life force energy in the English language, but in Indian culture, its equivalent is *'prana'* and in Chinese culture it is known as *'chi'*.

As the sexual energy charge builds during lovemaking, we increase our access to this basic life force. Sex offers a way to cultivate and use life force energy for other purposes: giving and receiving pleasure, physical and emotional healing, creating love, and excelling in other areas of human endeavour such as science, business, the arts, and sports.

3. Sexuality is a legitimate spiritual path. Tantra is also yoga because the word 'yoga' means union. Tantric yoga includes the union of sexuality and spirituality.

Sex and spirit are not two separate aspects of our selves, On the contrary, spiritual lovemaking is one of the simplest ways for ordinary people to experience mystical connection — union with themselves, their partners, and the Divine.

The arbitrary separation of body, mind, and spirit in most cultures is an intellectual, psychological, and emotional tragedy. This error of judgement has been the cause of great suffering for countless generations of people. It is now time for healing that can only be possible by reuniting sexuality and spirituality. My belief is that the time of Tantra has arrived.

4. We are each responsible for our own sexual fulfilment as well as our own personal and spiritual growth. Despite popular belief, it is not your lover's job to bring you to sexual ecstasy. No matter how attentive or skilful your lover may be, unless you allow yourself to open fully to sexual pleasure, you will not reach the heights of orgasmic bliss.

Anxiety of results or performance is one of the killers of passionate sexual intimacy. When we each take responsibility for our own sexual pleasure and our own spiritual awakening, the pressure to perform in either is eliminated.

Tantra also states that together as partners you can help and assist each other on the path, combining your energies, thus making the path to your own completion smoother and faster.

My spiritual master was known by different people for different things. Some thought of him to be an accomplished yogi, others thought of him as a master of ancient Vedantic thought. Still others knew him as the master of the secret science of Sri-Vidya, and some followed him as the one who carried the lineage of the tradition of the Himalayan masters. Few, if any, knew him as a master of the way of life called Tantra. In reality he was all this, and much more.

My life, and evolution of my soul, brought me to him for one reason and one reason only, I believe. As I was growing up, I instinctively knew that the sexual energy within us was a manifestation of the divine life force within us. In other words, for me, the energy of sexuality felt within was an expression and extension of the divinity within, not separate or opposed to it.

From my childhood, two subjects, sexuality and spirituality, fascinated me. Superficially seeming to be diametrically opposite, to me they appeared as the two points of the same circle. I was searching, without conscious thought, for a path that would merge the two.

I realized that to ignore or negate any one of the two would mean one could climb the highest mountain but still remain a step away from the summit. It was only in merging these two energies, that total completeness and one-ness could be achieved.

Tantra was my way, and I recognized it as such the moment I was exposed to it for the first time. It was almost as if the knowledge and understanding long lost in the recesses of my being came flooding back to me.

I am eternally grateful to my spiritual master for giving me the gift of Tantra.

I wrote this book to take you for a walk through the garden of your senses, to arrive at your own consciousness.

Our five senses, powerful and yet so subtle, embedded in us by existence, are the creation of universal energy and are gifted to us to connect us with the world we live in. Imagine what life would be like without our senses.

Just as the senses connect you to the world around you, you can also use them to connect totally with your partner in the act of loving.

With this connection you can become one with the consciousness of the Universe around you.

Open your senses totally... walk through this garden of sensual life totally. If you do so, you will realize that you have arrived at your own spirit.

Smell, taste, touch, see and hear your partner totally. Intuit their wishes, needs, and desires. Become one with her consciousness.

Breathe in life in all its totality and give yourself fully as you breathe out love with every heartbeat.

As a Tantric master once said to me with a sly smile, 'Tantra is not about making love with a woman. Through her as a goddess, you make love to the whole Universe.'

Tantra is about becoming whole and total. Tantra is about making love to existence itself.

Welcome to a path full of pleasure that will take you to the ultimate realization of Unity, One-ness and Divinity. You will arrive at this juncture through the union of your body, the vehicle that has been created by thousands of years of evolution just for this very experience, with that of your lover.

Tantra unites bodies, minds, hearts and souls.

It makes the two into one.

I wish you a sex-citing journey.

Vikas Malkani

1

Intuit

'To be so utterly in the present moment that no anxiety, pain and suffering, and fear, can survive, is your true nature, your real state of Being'

Advice from a Tantric Master

Tantra is the Art of Spiritualising Sexuality. It offers practical tools to transmute fear and attachment into love. Tantra is the letting go of all mental, emotional and cultural conditioning. Tantra is total surrender to what *is* so that universal life energy can again flow through us like a river without effort.

The word Tantra has many definitions. Some scholars claim it comes from the Sanskrit or Hindi word for fabric or tapestry, meaning that it is woven into one's life.

Others say that it comes from two Sanskrit words — tanoti and trayati. Tanoti means to expand consciousness, and trayati means to liberate consciousness.

Tantra Expands and Liberates Consciousness, Making it the Fabric of Existence.

As the highest possible synthesis between love and meditation, Tantra is the connection between this and other planes of existence.

While not a religious philosophy, Tantra embraces a deep spiritual understanding of life, and an ancient art of living in harmony with yourself, and with others.

It is a poetic science of sexuality that dates back thousands of years — it was used as a vehicle to achieve cosmic consciousness and union with divinity.

Tantra treats sexual energy as a loving friend rather than something to be suppressed or talked about secretly. It does not deny sex, or consider sex a hindrance to enlightenment.

Tantrics are god loving, rather than god-fearing. Tantra doesn't tell you to suppress your sexual urges to reach god, but just the opposite; it supports development of this vital energy to achieve union with divinity.

It is the ultimate *yoga* — a Sanskrit word for union.

In Tantra the orgasm is with the universe. You become part of the primal energy of everything — and merge your individuality with the Absolute.

The Tantra vision accepts everything. There is nothing forbidden in Tantra. Everything that a person experiences, regardless of whether it is usually judged as good or bad, is an opportunity for learning. For instance, a situation in which you feel sexually frustrated is not viewed negatively in Tantra, but as a teaching. It provides an opportunity to understand your motivations about going into sex. What does it mean to you? When have you repeated this pattern of behaviour in the past? Why you are tolerating the situation? What opportunities for change are available to you? Through this questioning you can develop a sense of how to make your sex life work better. This vision can guide you as a blueprint for the kind of experiences that you wish to create for yourself.

In Tantra there is no division between what is good and what is bad, what is acceptable and what is unacceptable. Tantra places no moral judgement on your sexual preferences. In Tantra the focus is not so much on with whom you do it but rather on how you do it. Hence, Tantra can be practised by anyone.

The Tantra vision is one of wholeness, of embracing everything, because every situation, whether pleasant or unpleasant, is an opportunity to become more aware about who you are and how you can expand your capacities. And this provides a great opportunity for integrating all aspects of yourself including those parts that you may normally reject or hide. This vision also recognizes that within each adult human being there is a natural, unspoiled, childlike spirit which can openly and innocently explore unfamiliar territory. The innocence of this spirit remains intact and represents our natural capacity to enjoy life, to love, to play and to be ecstatic.

Because Tantra believes in wholeness, it embraces opposites, seeing them not as contradictions but as complements. The concepts of male and female are not set apart, forever divided by a gender gap, but are viewed as two polarities that meet and merge in every human being. Tantra recognizes that each human being, whether man or woman has both masculine and feminine qualities.

In Tantra the man is encouraged to explore his soft, receptive, vulnerable, feminine aspects. He can slip out from beneath the weight of his male responsibilities, stop performing and relax, taking his time in sex, making love without a specific goal, allowing himself to receive while his partner initiates.

For her part, the woman can explore her masculine dimension, recognizing that she is capable of dynamic leadership in lovemaking, taking the initiative, creating new ways of guiding, teaching, and giving herself and her partner pleasure. The man does not give up his masculinity, nor does the woman abandon her feminity. They simply expand their potential to include the other polarity.

In Tantra, When the Male and Female Polarities Merge, a New Dimension Becomes Available — the Sense of the Sacred.

When the sacredness of sexual union is felt, it is possible to experience your connection to the life force itself, the source of creation. This connection lifts your consciousness beyond the physical plane into a field of power and energy to everything that lives and loves. You feel that you are a part of the great dance of existence, you feel one with it.

Introducing a sacred dimension to sexual loving allows both partners to acknowledge that they possess divine qualities. They recognize their true potential as infinite and unlimited. In Tantra you discover that by honouring the god or goddess in your partner, you can see beyond the limitations of personality and, by seeing the divine in the other person, perceive the same potential in yourself. The other person becomes a reflection of your own godlike nature. That is why Tantric partners greet each other by saying, 'I honour you as an aspect of myself.' This means, 'You are one with me, and your consciousness is a reflection of mine.'

When we learn the erotic arts in this way, a deep healing of our sexuality takes place. The sex act is not hurried and tense affair, fraught with the dangers of disease (transmitted by partners who do not take time for thorough preparations), but a safe and healthy exchange between partners who respect and know each other intellectually, emotionally, and sensually before they enter into sexual union.

According to Tantra, sex is first a matter of energy, and then of physical action. Tantra views energy as the movement of life and recognizes that within the human body, energy is continuously in motion.

The nucleus and electrons of an atom have characteristic vibratory movements and rhythms. The same goes for the molecules, cells, and organs of the human body. Each cell in the body pulsates rhythmically, and so do the heart, diaphragm, intestines, lungs, brain, and many other physiological components. The vibrations from these rhythmic movements generate bioelectrical currents that stream continuously through the whole body. They also generate energy fields that surround the body, and our moods and emotions generate specific vibrations that alter these energy fields as well.

Tantra sees each human being as an organism that is part of a larger whole — the surrounding environment, the planet Earth, nature itself — in which rhythm and vibration are the unifying factors. They are also the factors that influence the relationship of one person to another. So Tantra teaches lovers how to harmonize their energies and be on the same wavelength, creating a measurable resonance between their energy fields.

In Tantra the art of creating such a resonance is equivalent to what we call foreplay.

One of the deepest insights of Tantra is that the human body is a single energy phenomenon. At one end of the spectrum, at the physical level, this energy is expressed as the sex drive. At the other end of the spectrum, at the level of the nervous system and the brain, energy is experienced as ecstasy. The sexual drive is instinctual, raw, unrefined energy. Tantra believes that this same sexual drive can be transformed and refined into ecstasy. But it is a single energy manifesting itself in different ways. Sexual energy is therefore to be accepted and respected as the raw material — the crude oil from which the high-octane fuel of ecstasy is produced.

Tantra believes that the earliest Eastern mystics obtained their first glimpses of spiritual enlightenment at the moment of orgasm. Indeed, many people know that orgasm can temporarily transport them to a state of rapture. For a few seconds the mind becomes devoid of thought, the individualistic, egocentric view of life disappears, and se step outside of time into the timeless now of bliss.

So sex, to the early mystics, was the very source of the religious experience, as it can still be today, given the right attitude and conditions.

Making Love is a Spiritual Experience

In the ancient texts of China and India it is written that it was common for emperors, kings and noblemen trained in the art of lovemaking to be passionate lovers in their nineties with up to twenty consorts, all of whom they were keeping sexually satisfied.

In the ruling class a man's power was measured by the number of consorts he could keep satisfied. A husband was respected more for keeping his wife sexually satisfied than for anything else. In the ancient cultures of Egypt, Arabia, India, Nepal, Tibet, China and Japan, polygamy was common, so it was essential for a man to know the arts of lovemaking.

In Chinese Taoist texts it is written that the emperor should make love to nine chosen consorts every night, progressing from the lower ranks to the higher. An ancient Chinese text says: 'Retaining his semen by proficiency in the Art of Love, the Emperor concentrates powers within. Then, at the full moon, he bestows his seed on the Queen of Heaven.' A child born from such a ritual was purported to have magical powers.

Most men these days ejaculate within the first ten minutes of being engaged in lovemaking, and wouldn't have commanded much respect in ancient China. Our education and proficiency in the art of lovemaking is lacking in our modern day, yet every man has the ability to master these sexual skills.

Ancient texts from East teach that sex is sacred. I like the idea of my lovemaking being sacred. I don't use the term sacred here in the conventional religious sense of something existing above us somewhere. Such a view tends to split reality into two parts, with a degraded Earth below and a pure Heaven on high. Things on this earthly plane can be sacred if we have the eyes to see the sacredness in them: the sacred relationship of Earth and sky, of life and death, of the mind and the heart and the body. We can view human existence itself as sacred, and, if we choose, see lovemaking as sacred.

Many people today are seeking spiritual growth; spiritual understanding and progress while living in this real world of relationships, career and responsibility. When I tell them that they can use sexual love as a way of becoming more spiritual they are quite shocked at times. This probably stems from the fact that many religions proclaim that if we want to become spiritual we must deny our earthly pleasures.

A mystical, or spiritual, experience is foreign to most Westerners. A mystical state is not easy to describe, and yet anyone who has had the experience recognizes it. People describe certain common elements in mystical experience, such as a sense of tranquility, of timelessness, of intense awareness that everything you see is vivid and everything you touch is very alive; a transcendence from the thoughts of daily life; an expansion of consciousness; a feeling of being connected with the cosmos or at unity with all things. Some say they have a tangible experience of God; others experience the bliss of union with the Divine.

Some of these elements can also be present during lovemaking; and when they are it is important to acknowledge this as a spiritual experience. Being in a heightened orgasmic state is a mystical experience. Ancient spiritual systems such as Tantra and Taoism readily acknowledge this.

Tantra, a spiritual science from ancient India, and Taoism, from ancient China, are similar in their basic essence. Both involve balancing the male and female energies to create harmony and both have an ultimate goal of spiritual unity with the universe or the source or the God within.

The Tantric interplay of the male and female energies was represented in ancient Hindu mythology by Shiva and Shakti and in Taoism by yin and yang. Both Tantra and Taoism aim to create union of body, mind, and spirit. In both traditions sexuality is seen and practised in a spiritual content, and is a means to an end, not the end in itself. Sexuality is meant to take us to spirituality.

One of the differences between Tantra and Taoism is that Tantra is filled with mystical rituals and practices, whereas Taoism is more scientific in its approach. People who are more intuitive or right-brain oriented would likely be more attracted to Tantra, while those who are more rational and logical, more left-brain oriented, would likely be attracted to Taoism, although this is certainly not a rule. As men open their heart centres more and become deeply connected with their women, they move forward into the Tantric approach to sexuality.

It is said that Tantra is the oldest single source of knowledge concerning the energies of the mind, body and spirit. It is the origin and essence of yoga, martial arts, t'ai chi, and the grand philosophies of the Buddha, Confucius, and Lao-Tzu. It is even believed that the teachings of the Tao sprang up from the wisdom of Tantra.

The word Tantra has many interpretations and in one sense also means 'to expand', 'to be free' and 'to be liberated'.

If we are to be really free our sexuality should not be repressed; it should be lived in its totality with joy and without guilt. The more we suppress our sexual desires, the more we will be bound by those desires; the more our sexuality is repressed; the more it wants to burst out. The sad thing is that repressed sexuality often bursts out in harmful ways.

Tantra teaches that to know the truth about love, you need to accept the sacredness of sex. It teaches that there should be no repression or guilt attached to sex. It also teaches that when a man approaches his beloved he should carry a feeling of the sacred, as if he were stepping in to a temple.

Through the centuries many mainstream religions have frowned on Tantra and Taoism because both systems use sexual union as a vehicle to enlightenment, as a way of experiencing a deep connection with God, the cosmos, the Divine or the source of all existence. Most religious systems make sex taboo, claiming it leads people away from God. This predominant religious approach eventually forced Tantric practices underground, where they have been kept secret for hundreds of years.

Only recently, in the past 50 years, have Tantric and Taoist practices been interpreted, published and made available for general study. This has been refreshing and enlightening for many of us because it has helped us to look at love and sex from a different prospective. We start to question our own attitudes and realize how deeply our consciousness has been conditioned by our religious and cultural upbringing, which suggests that sexuality is somehow un-clean.

The Tantric attitude toward sex is that sex is God's greatest gift; that it is sacred; that to have pleasure from sex is a prayer to God; a way of showing gratitude for our existence.

Tantra sees sexual union as a way of generating life force through the body that is healing, rejuvenating and energizing. It can be used as a meditation to reach mystical states of love and consciousness.

Because Tantra covers the full spectrum of life it accepts and reveres sexual love and pleasure. It does not accept any kind of religious, cultural, or tribal inhibitions, It's about exploring the extraordinary in your love and your sexuality, with the only condition being that it causes the other person or yourself no harm.

Tantra preaches that we deserve all the love and sexual pleasure we can possibly receive; that sexual loving is a way to reach the mysteries of the heart, the soul, the god and goddess within each person. It also teaches that sex is a way of bonding with a lover — physically, emotionally and spiritually — to create feelings of ecstatic pleasure, deep intimacy and expanded consciousness. It's a way of transcending daily life and the ego to become one with your beloved, to become one with all things, and to invite a tangible experience of God.

Tantra says that lovemaking is the way to longevity and that by applying certain techniques we can rejuvenate ourselves and awaken our immense centres. It also believes that we can use our lovemaking to heal ourselves and our partners, because when we are in heightened states of sexual energy our whole body is charged and the immune system strengthened.

But what does Tantra have to say about what one is to do when intense desire troubles you and you just cannot control it?

First of all, you must understand that the sexual drive isn't in the least negative. It is part of our being embodied. It is as natural as any other bodily function. There is nothing obscene about it, and all the bad feelings we might possibly have are simply learned and conditioned responses, all of which arise from the past. They are inappropriate responses and so you need not be concerned about them at all.

Second, you must simply accept that you are feeling sexual. In fact, allow yourself to really feel those feelings in your body. Instead of immediately creating a problem for yourself by dreaming up ways of fulfiling the sexual urge, simply sit with those feelings for a while; welcome them like a good friend; notice the excitement you feel and understand that you don't have to do anything about those sensations, other than accept and notice them as fully as you can. Generally, what happens then is that the sexual excitement spreads as a warm, tingling sensation over other parts of the body and ceases to be troubling.

Third, you can assist this process of sexual transfusion by breathing. Breathing is probably the most important practice discovered by yogis, and mystics, Controlled breathing is probably the most direct way of regulating the body's life force. Breathing is like the outer shell of the subtle psychosomatic energy called *prana* in Hinduism and *chi* in Taoism.

Fourth, understand yourself. What are your most profound goals? If you truly, truly aspire to a life devoted to spiritual growth, you will have to accept a measure of discipline, including sexual discipline. You need not necessarily become a celibate, but you will have to cultivate new attitudes toward everything, including your attitude toward sexual gratification.

In traditions, like Tantra and Taoism, the idea is to actively conduct the sexual energy into the body as a whole, especially toward the crown of the head, where an important psychic centre is located. The transmuted sexual energy is thought to break open the door to the higher Self, the Atman, beyond the ego personality. It is the dragon that can help us soar to the greater heights, or that can devour us if we are not wise. Sexuality is a tremendous force.

In the words of Osho — a famous spiritual Master well known for his liberated views on sex and spirituality, 'Sex is the only energy you have got. The energy can be transformed — it can become a higher energy. The higher it moves the less and less sexuality remains in it. And there is an end peak where it becomes simply love and compassion. The ultimate we can call divine energy, but the base, remains sex. So sex is the first, bottom layer of energy — and God is the top layer. But the same energy moves. You cannot kill it. No energy can be killed — energy can only be transformed. There is no way to destroy energy. Nothing can be destroyed in this world, it can only be transformed, changed, moved into a new realm and dimension. Destruction is impossible. You cannot create a new energy and you cannot destroy an old energy. Creation and destruction cannot be done. Now, scientists agree to this — not even a single atom can be destroyed.

'For two thousand years, religion consisted of becoming absolutely without sex. That created a struggle because the more your suppress, the more sexual you become. And then sex moves deeper into the unconscious. It poisons your whole being. Sex has to be transformed, neither repressed nor madly indulged. And the only possible way to transform sex is to be sexual with deep meditative awareness. Move into sex, but with an alert, conscious, mindful being. Don't allow it to become an unconscious force. Don't be pulled and pushed by it. Move knowingly, understandingly, lovingly. Make sexual experience a meditative experience. Meditate in it. This is what the East has done through Tantra.'

The above is an apt description of how we make sex spiritual, of how we merge sex with the spirit. To understand the spiritual significance of sex energy, whether one can and should sublimate and spiritualize sex, and is it even possible to make love as a meditation, read on. Hear the words of the mystic Osho, once again, as he delves into the real significance and purpose of the sexual energy in man.

'There is no such thing as sex energy. Energy is one and the same. Sex is one outlet for it, one direction for it; it is one of the applications of the energy. Life energy is one, but it can manifest in many directions. Sex is one of them. When life energy becomes biological, it becomes sex energy. Sex is just an application of the life energy. So there is no question of sublimation. If life energy flows in another direction, there is no sex. But it is not a sublimation; it is a transformation. Sex is the natural, biological flow of life energy, and the lowest application of it. It is natural because life cannot exist without it, and the lowest because it is the foundation not the peak. When sex becomes the totality, the whole life is just a waste. It is like laying a foundation and going on laying the foundation, without ever building the house for which the foundation is meant. Sex is just an opportunity for a higher transformation of life energy.'

Tantric Meditations

At the end of each chapter I offer one meditation technique to help people experience Tantra and understand its basic principles. There is no special sequence of exercises, or step-by-step progression. To me, Tantra is an insight and a revelation, not a simple training. It is a discovery of something that already exists, both within you and in nature. Each technique will give you a different taste of Tantra. In this way, by the end of the book, your understanding will be rooted in personal experience.

There are a few simple things you can do to enhance your experience of these Tantric techniques. For example, you can create a special meditation space or temple in your home that is used only for these exercises. If a whole room is not available, you can temporarily transform a living room, study or bedroom into a Tantra temple, using incense, lighting and soft background music. This will give more significance to the time you devote to your exploration of Tantra and your experiences will be deepened accordingly. Try to make sure that you will not be disturbed, either by phone calls, other people in the house, or loud music and television. This will help you to focus on the exercises with more totality. It is also helpful to take shower before starting and to wear something fresh, loose and comfortable.

Tantric Meditation 1

Connect with Each Other Through the Breath.

Breath is one of the easiest and most effective ways to feel connected with another person. When two people are deeply in love it happens by itself: sitting or lying together, they naturally start breathing in the same rhythm. Being in love, they are already in harmony, merging with each other, so naturally their breathing becomes harmonious as well. The same phenomenon can happen consciously and deliberately. Just by taking time to sit together and tune your breathing, a connection is formed.

- The man sits with his back against a wall with his legs stretched out and open. The woman sits closely in front of him, facing in the same direction, gently resting her back against the man's chest.
- Take a few moments to get comfortable.
- Close your eyes and bring your attention to your own breathing, allowing it to become slow and relaxed. Breathe into your belly.
- When you are ready, without hurry or effort, the man tunes into the woman's breathing and follows her rhythm for ten minutes. When your beloved breathes out, you breathe out. When your beloved breathes in, you breathe in.
- Almost immediately, you will feel linked, connected. You will discover that this is an easy and natural way to create a feeling of harmony and togetherness.

Then, when you are ready for the next stage, the woman follows the man's breathing for ten minutes. After this, you can let go of any idea about who is following whom, and simply fall in tune with each other's breathing. You can do this exercise for 30 minutes or longer if it feels good to do so. There is nowhere to go and nothing to do. You can simply employ this form of communion. After some time, if you wish, you can slowly move out of this position, come together and begin to make love while staying in harmony with your breathing.

There will be moments when you lose the connection, but that is perfectly okay. Once you have come together, you can re-establish the rhythm. Continue for as long as you like, either making love or lying together in a quiet embrace. You will be surprised at how much intimacy can be created through this simple technique.

Advanced Tantric Meditation 1

Disappearing into Dance

This is one of the most simple and yet beautiful meditation techniques, based on the Hindu concept of God as a dancer.

In this sense, God is not seen as a creator, like an artist painting a picture, or a sculptor carving a rock, but as a continuous expression of creativity — more like a dancer. The difference is profound: unlike the painter and the sculptor, there is no separation between the dancer and the dance. The two can only exist together in creative motion.

The whole point of this meditation is to lose oneself in the dance, to dance madly, wildly, ecstatically, so that only the dance remains. This brings you to a point of inner awareness where you experience that you are not the body. The body goes on moving but you are out of it, beyond it. And this can also be fun: dancing is not a serious activity.

* Find a nice space in which to dance.
* Make sure that for one hour you will not be disturbed.
* Wear loose clothes that will not inhibit your movements.

* Choose your favourite dance music and arrange it so that you can dance continuously, without interruption for forty minutes.
* Begin the meditation, dancing wildly.
* When the music ends, lie down on the floor, completely relaxed, for twenty minutes. Just be a witness to any body sensations, any feelings, any thoughts. Let everything be as it is.

2

Hear

'Surrender. Surrender to what is. Surrender is neither passivity nor resignation. Surrender is yielding to life, to become aware of its natural rhythm, rather than fighting against it. Surrender is 'going with the flow of life itself, not trying to swim against the current.'

Advice from a Tantric Master

Freud onwards, psychology has conceded that the sexual drive or energy can be transformed into higher avenues such as art and spirituality.

Erich Fromm wrote in *The Art of Loving* that the basic for our need to love lies in the experience of separateness and the resulting need to overcome the anxiety of separateness by the experience of union. In its deepest meaning then love/sex becomes spiritual. However, even in the 21st century, this fundamental mystery of life has remained unsolved; neither understood nor accepted. Sex is still shrouded in a mist of shame, guilt, fear, curiosity, attraction, repulsion, intoxication and helplessness, due in no small measure to the teachings of our many misinterpreted and mis-represented religions and philosophies.

Just mention the word 'sex' and you see people change to become defensive, shameful and guilty. Or you see them lean forward with great interest. What is the lure of sex? What is it about the act of making love that captures everyone's attention like no other desire? Is it a momentary experience of bliss, of pure pleasure? Or is it a taste, a glimpse of timelessness, limitlessness, ego-less-ness, selflessness that grabs hold of us and refuses to let go? And if the result of the act of union between two opposite energies in man and woman is so great and profound, why does the whole world insist on suppressing, ignoring or debasing it?

If we delve deep into the history of humanity, we find that for the past many thousand years, around the planet, in every civilization and culture, sex has been a taboo. In all the civilizations whether Chinese, Indian, Greek, Roman, Egyptian or Babylonian — sex was the forbidden fruit.

Interestingly, the more supposedly cultured and civilized the race was, the more sex was unacceptable to it. And the more it was denied openly, the more it was indulged in secretly. Whereas the so-called uncivilised, uncultured societies had a natural and uninhibited sexual life that simply rejoiced in the rhythm and music of two bodies pulsating in tune with each other. These so-called uncultured people — the tribal and the aboriginal, who still live in harmony with nature — have no inhibitions about sex and nudity.

With culture, the embarrassment about one's naked body and the denial of our raw animal instincts crept in. The most discomforting feature of the sex act is that, while making love, man has to slide down the ladder of evolution and become pure animal if he wants to enjoy vigorous and passionate intercourse with his partner. This encounter with one's own intense animal state is extremely frightening.

When the sexual force is not understood as spiritual or sacred, sex is considered to be a purely physical, instinctual drive and as a result not held in reverence. Rather, it is sometimes misused as it becomes associated with personal power and conquest — the dominance of one gender over another. Deprived of its sacred dimension, sexual energy is repressed and eventually directed against life itself. This, in turn, results in disrespect, disease, abuse, rape and other forms of sexual violence.

Negative social conditioning about sex inevitably creates fear, and well-intentioned instruments such as parents, teachers and religion pass this fear from generation to generation. In early childhood, most of us absorb condemnatory attitudes about sex without even becoming aware of the process. This conditioning cripples our spontaneity, our expression of sexual vitality, our pleasure, and our ability to love and honour one another.

Fear also inhibits communication sex. Instead of being a process of deep communion between two people, lovemaking often becomes a tense encounter in which both partners are afraid to express their real needs.

The fundamental view pervading the contemporary spiritual scene seems to be that sex, long seen as the enemy of the spirit, is actually its ally, or can be made to act like one. This sex-positive spiritual view holds that to truly become whole, we must free our sexuality from the chains of guilt, shame and repression and allow it to find full expression as a natural, healthy and even sacred part of life.

This belief has become so widespread that today; the spiritual practice of celibacy — considered for millennia to be a profound, powerful and even crucial aspect of spiritual life by Christians, Buddhists and Hindus alike — seems to have all but fallen by the wayside. The modern consensus seems to be that in a psychologically enlightened culture, celibacy no longer has much relevance.

It is time now to look at sex with fresh eyes, to add meditation to sex, which means adding more awareness to your sexual craving and in the process, purifying it. To cleanse sex of its moral, legal, social and emotional conditioning. To make friends with your body, which has as much wisdom as the mind.

It is important to stress that we are all sexual beings, coming into existence through an act of sex — you cannot deny the truth of your sexual nature.

Sex is only the first step in man's spiritual journey, not the last. Finally, the way to transcend sex forever is through it, not away from it. Otherwise, the transcendence is only transitory.

So, let us begin by accepting our own reality. There are two undeniable biological facts that we live with. First, we are born with genitals. Second, when stimulated they give us considerable pleasure. These two facts have been of perennial concern to religious authorities.

While religious authorities have never been able to deny the fact that our bodies have genitals, they traditionally have paid a disproportionate amount of attention to what we are supposed to do with them.

At one end of the religious spectrum is the view that sexual activity is not really desirable beyond procreation, but that people, weak as they are, cannot be obliged to practice celibacy. At the other end of the spectrum are the body and sex positive schools of Eastern esotericism, such as Tantra and Taoism.

In opposition to what is often believed about these Oriental approaches of Tantra and Taoism, they do not endorse the pursuit of pleasure for its own sake.

Tantra is definitely not hedonism. Tantric exercises are not primarily about feeling good, though feeling good is certainly not considered a sin either. Tantra and other comparable traditions are primarily about transcending the ego and realizing the larger whole.

These schools do not deny pleasure. What they ask us to do is to deepen pleasure until we find the transcendental bliss in it. Conventional pleasure, they say, is always accompanied with a degree of pain, partly because it is finite and varyingly intense, and partly because when enjoyed in excess it can lead to physical and psychic suffering.

By contrast, the transcendental bliss, *ananda,* as experienced in the state of ecstatic self-transcendence, is complete in itself and is utterly satisfying to our whole being. It signals the end of all psychic suffering. Whereas in the wake of pleasure, displeasure is sure to follow, bliss has no shadow side. It always nourishes and sustains our being.

As far as abstinence and celibacy are concerned, yoga students will be familiar with the Sanskrit expression *brahmacharya,* which is the age-old ideal of celibacy within the Hindu tradition. This practice is embedded in an understanding of the esoteric processes that occur during sublimation. This esoteric knowledge is useful even to those who do not wish to live a long-term celibate life, so I give you a brief overview below.

The word *brahmacharya* actually means 'Brahmic conduct'. This can be interpreted as meaning the conduct of a Brahmin, a member of the priestly class of Hindu society, or the conduct that is in accordance with the Brahman, the Absolute or Universal Reality. The Brahman is conceived as beyond space and time and hence beyond all differentiation, including gender distinctions. It is sexless. The person practising *brahmacharya,* seeks to emulate the sexless nature of the Absolute. In so doing, it is said, he or she acquires the same form as the Absolute. In other words, he or she becomes enlightened, freed from the limitations of the ego-personality.

It is clear from the classical descriptions of the *brahmacharin* or *brahmacharini* (if female) that he or she is no weakling. On the contrary, this chastity generates great psycho-physical power.

The Hindus understood earlier and better than anyone else than the preservation of sexual energy can, if rightly done, serve as rich fuel for the spiritual process. The body has a hidden mechanism for converting sexual energy into something that is both more subtle and more potent, and that can act as a force for breaking open the gateway to the ultimate union, the ecstatic consciousness of *samadhi.*

Without knowledge of this occult process however, the student of yoga and spirituality is like a blind person. It is important that the yoga practitioner understands what is happening in the laboratory of the body as a result of the preservation and regulation of the sexual energy.

According to the classical accounts, whenever the male semen is emitted, it involves a loss of valuable energy. We can understand this as a loss of hormones that might otherwise be utilized in the chemistry of the body to nourish organs, notably the brain. But the yogic masters insist that there is something more important involved here. They claim that semen, which is continually generated by the gonads, invigorates our psycho-mental life through the agency of what they call *ojas.* This *ojas* is a subtle energy that rises from the sexual centre to the brain. It is the product of a process of continuous transmutation that occurs in the genitals when the semen is preserved. *Ojas* is a force that is not unique to men. Female yogini, or women, can also preserve their sexual charge and transmute it for higher purposes.

In some extraordinary states of consciousness, this alchemical process that happens spontaneously can actually be seen in inner vision. The late Gopi Krishna, an adept from Kashmir, whose works on Kundalini Yoga are widely read, offered this description:

'There can be no doubt whatsoever that the incessant, easily perceptible, rapid movement at the base of my spine... was an indication of the fact that a hidden organ had begun to function all of a sudden in the hitherto innocent looking region, converting the reproductive fluid into a radiant essence of high potency which, racing along the nerve fibers as well as the spinal canal, nourished the brain and the organs with the rejuvenating substance out of reach in any other way.'

Gopi Krishna speculated that a new psychosomatic centre was in the process of forming in his brain as a result of his accidental awakening of the 'serpent-power' or *kundalini-shakti.* This kundalini is conceived as being normally latent in the human body. Upon its arousal it revolutionizes the chemistry of the body, leading to psychic states and, ultimately, enlightenment. According to Gopi Krishna's understanding, this newly forming centre in his brain was drawing energy from the genital region.

There is no scientific evidence for what Gopi Krishna saw happening in his own body, but this does not necessarily say anything about Gopi Krishna or his experience. More likely, it merely reflects the bias and ignorance of contemporary science. What Gopi Krishna has shared with us in his books has been known for centuries in India, Tibet, China and elsewhere wherever men and women have dedicated their lives to explore the vast regions of consciousness.

It is revealing to read in an ancient Hindu Scripture thousands of years old attributed to Lord Shiva, the lord of all yoga: 'Sex is an awesome force that can either rejuvenate or debilitate, depending on whether it is practised correctly or incorrectly.'

From Sex to Enlightenment

Imagine how much more we could embrace our sexuality if we were introduced to such beliefs as Tantra and Taoism when we first asked questions about sex. It's important to recognize that any judgements we have about sex reflect our inhibitions and demonstrate that we are not entirely free and accepting of our own sexuality.

Some aspects of Tantra and Taoism may appear a little strange at first, especially the link between sexuality and spirituality, but like anything in life we need to consider all approaches and then select what serves us. Of course, sometimes when a new attitude is presented to us we take it on immediately because it rings true for us. At other times we have to let it sit for a while; we put it on the shelf and perhaps use it in years to come, It's important to experiment, to play with innocence and openness as a child plays with a new toy. I believe it's time to choose new ways of exploring sex and love on physical, emotional and spiritual levels.

Now here is a great truth for you — having a healthy attitude toward lovemaking makes all the difference to the experience. You can be in exactly the same lovemaking position as someone else, but ultimately it's the mind that creates the experience. If the mind is saying, 'I wish this would end,' you may have some sort of resistance to pleasure from past conditioning. How could the most sensitive part of the body, with the most nerve endings, not give you pleasure? If you believe that to make love to reach high states of sexual pleasure is healing, then the experience will be totally different. Our experience of lovemaking is affected by our attitudes. A man who has been conditioned to believe that lovemaking is a spiritual encounter will have a totally different experience from a man who sees it as an opportunity to feel better through conquest.

Anything that happens in our lovemaking is interpreted first through our attitudes and beliefs. From these we derive our experience. One way to alter our experience is to change our attitudes and beliefs. Some people watching a high Tantric experience might see it merely as two people having good sex. So what is the difference between Tantra and just having great sex? One of the key differences is where the mind is focused at the moment. It's the same in life. One's experience of life depends on where the mind is. We are all living in the same world, but our differing experiences are determined by our perceptions.

In lovemaking it's not what we are doing that affects us; it's the attitude with which we are doing it that makes the real difference to our experience. If we can internalize the attitude that our lovemaking is spiritual, then our lovemaking will indeed become a spiritual experience.

There is definitely a connection between sex and the spirit. Depending on your attitude, making love can become a giving, expressing selfless act, which is a form of prayer in itself. Through the body, hearts can be touched, emotions opened, needs and desires expressed, fears released, security given and souls merged. Through the act of physical sharing, the Divine in us can be revered and remembered. Making love can go from the physical to the emotional and finally to a spiritual level where it becomes a prayer to the Divine.

Empowering your Sexual Self

When sex is good, it can be taken for granted, but when it's bad it can consume much of the consciousness of a relationship. As one of life's most exceptional pleasures, it's ironic that there are so many hidden obstacles to sexual fulfilment. Such as the 'ageing sex life' stereotypes — the notion that sex is no longer great or frequent by age 45 or 60 or beyond. These myths persist despite recent studies showing couples in their eighties enjoying sex regularly. Trapped by misconceptions, few of us ever come close to realizing our life-long potential for sexual energy, nor do we comprehend our capacity for extraordinary sexual pleasures and deeply satisfying intimacy.

There is a growing awareness that great sex is not something that just happens, it comes no more naturally than great communication. It has to be learned in a shared, sensitive, open manner. What's emerging from scientific studies is a whole new model of human sexuality, one that emphasizes pleasure, closeness, and self and partner-enhancement rather than 'performance'. Few of life's experiences yield greater rewards, since as our intimate relationships become more vibrant and aware, so in turn do we.

The energy of desire resides, and is nourished or confounded, in the mind. Everyday, therapists worldwide treat countless cases of unwarranted anxiety and loss of sex drive in men and women. To a significant extent, the vanishing sexual energy and corresponding relationship struggles are brought on by popular misconceptions about sexual potency and intimacy. When we believe these erroneous ideas, we can end up sexually weakened by our own thoughts.

To truly understand the innate energy within our body and to bring it to full bloom, it is necessary to transcend these misconceptions and to renew our sexual power.

I offer you 10 powerful and practical solutions that have been arrived at by many experts.

Use them to your benefit.

1. Turn Sex into Love-play, Instead of Foreplay and The Act of Making Love. Unhurried, whole body love-play is a highly practical solution to both men's and women's primary complaints about the other's style of loving. Sensitive, sensual intimacy helps give men the aroused, responsive lovers they want, while at the same time it gives women more of the whole body sharing they often desire. Extended love-play means more variety, more playfulness and less likelihood of slipping into a boring routine.

'Touch may be the most powerful socio-biological signal of all', according to psycho-biologist Earnest Lawrence Rossi, PhD. 'When we are touched gently and rhythmically, our brains release the feel-good messenger chemicals called beta-endorphins, and we slip into the psychologically receptive state where we are open to increasing intimacy.'

Sigmund Freud may have initiated much of the present public confusion about the sensuality/sexuality link by postulating that the body contains only three erogenous zones (areas that lead to sexual arousal when stimulated): the mouth, anal area and genitals. The fact is, the entire body can respond with tip-to-toe erotic energy during lovemaking, so there's no reason to let your sensual powers lie dormant.

2. Take a Sensory Tour of Your Body with Your Sexual Partner. This simple technique, originating from the teachings of Tantra (and described in greater detail later in this book) can help create a greater feeling of shared trust and a sensual and emotional bond between lovers. It can also heighten sexual energy during intercourse. To develop exceptional skill in sensual and sexual touch, research has shown that one of the most effective exercises is the Sensory Body Tour.

First, choose a quiet, private room and choose a lighting level (bright, dim or dark) that is pleasing to both of you. If a certain smell arouses you (and is also enjoyed by your partner), create a hint of that scent in the room. If you both enjoy soft background music, put some on, Take the phone off the hook, put your favourite sheets on the bed and do whatever else you both wish to set the scene in the most enjoyable way.

Wearing as little or as much as you like, guide your partner's hands with your own on a special tour of every square inch of your body, showing him or her precisely the ways in which you like to be touched. Move in response to whatever touches you find most erotic, stimulating and desirable. If you or your partner enjoy whispered love messages, then be certain that that person receives them, but don't rely on the words and sound sensations alone to create erotic passion. Once you have covered every part of your body, switch places and let your lover guide you.

'Touch,' says Linda Perlin Alperstein, PhD, assistant clinical professor in Department of Psychiatry at the University of California, San Francisco, Medical Centre, 'can be difficult to discuss with words. It's much easier to demonstrate. You let your fingers do the talking. Of course, you can talk while conducting a Body Tour, but simple 'oohs' and 'ahhs' can be just as communicative as words... If you feel ill at ease naming certain parts of the body, the Body Tour allows you to show your partner how you like to be touched there without saying anything.'

Ancient Asian philosophers and physicians believed that exquisitely sensual, masterfully controlled sex replenished and strengthened the life force of both men and women. The prevailing idea was that sexual vitality and potency depended, first and foremost, on sensory awareness and sensual expertise.

3. Take Out Time to Leave Work and Other Stress Behind. If you arrive home from work and immediately dive into domestic chores, it's all but impossible to cultivate the level of intimacy that promotes extraordinary sex. You go from one type of stress to another. A practical suggestion is a five-minute transition period, a regular daily buffer zone time for couples to release work tensions and simply be together, to chat, stroll, hug, hold hands and perhaps sip a single glass of wine.

'A few minutes of peace and quiet can be worth four hours of foreplay,' says Dr Zilbergeld.

Another good suggestion is to meditate or pray together at specific times to break up your day into different parts. For example, when you are back from work, you could take a shower, and then sit quietly in meditation together before moving into the rest of the evening with each other.

4. Create an Atmosphere of Intimate Safety and Trust. Lasting intimacy and extraordinary sex depend at all times on a genuine sense of safety and trust. This requires that you and your partner be honest and clear with each other every time your are making sensual or sexual contact — not just in body but in your minds and shared words — about what pleases and what displeases or hurts.

Research indicates that extraordinary sex is only possible when both partners feel completely safe and trusting in letting go and deepening pleasures above and beyond orgasm instead of holding back, feeling unsafe and being unwilling to cross the boundaries in the mind or heart.

This requires sharpening your skills in listening to your inner signals and having confidence in discriminating between times when it's all right to feel emotionally or mentally or sexually vulnerable in lovemaking and times when it's not.

Limits can be gently set but must be firmly respected. A sense of safety also depends on the feeling that we, women and men, each create for ourselves by refusing to be involved with a partner who breaches our trust or will hurt us.

5. Ease your Mental Tensions. Distractions and anxieties arise in the mind and manifest themselves in your mood and body responses, and even when you may have the physical energy for sex, your ability to enjoy, really enjoy, lovemaking may be hindered by thoughts that make you anxious and interfere with or undermine your arousal.

Mental distractions, blue moods and fatigue all lower sexual energy and prevent many of us from getting in the lovemaking spirit or ruin sexual intimacy once we are close.

Clearly choose to enjoy lovemaking. Negative, unwanted thoughts thrive when the mind and mood are uncommitted to the experience of the moment. Make it clear to yourself that the sensual and sexual intimacy is something you desire right now and that you don't want to spoil it with worry, distracting thoughts or resentments.

When you find yourself mentally distracted during lovemaking, ask yourself, does this thought or image make me feel better? Or help me behave the way I want to? Or help me think productively about the situation? Or reinforce positive images I have about myself? Or improve my relationship?

'No matter what your problem or situation,' explains Dr Zilbergeld, 'there are always two ways to go with it. The negative way leads to discouragement, despair and self-hate. The more positive way leads to useful thinking, good feelings and solutions. Just because something hasn't been working lately doesn't mean it will never work. You can make changes.'

6. Focus on the Senses of Smell, Touch, Taste, Movement, Sight and Sound. Take a moment to remember what you have learned about the sensations that are most enjoyable and erotic to you and your partner. Keeping these preferences in mind, one of the simplest and most direct ways to light up sexual passion and disengage from mood swings or unwanted thoughts is to focus intently on the preferred sensations you are giving and receiving — the feelings of softness or warmth in your partner's touch; the sensations you get from skin touching skin, fingers stroking hair, lips on skin, tongue on skin or kissing in other erotic ways; the smoothness of the pillow or sheets; the movement of your chest as you breathe; the sound of intimate whisperings; the look of your lover's features that you find sexiest; the feeling of increased warmth in the body and the rhythm of muscles tightening and relaxing as you gradually increase the level of sensuality and intimacy.

7. Adopt what the Zen Masters Call 'Beginner's Mind'. To enjoy great sex, it's essential to suspend judgement for long enough to approach lovemaking in fresh, original, highly sensitive ways and to get out of ruts and routines as soon as they become so comfortable that your, or your partner's, sense of passion vanishes. This is called having the Beginner's Mind, and what the Tantric masters have long known as 'being total in the moment.'

Researchers have found that highly-sexual women have learned to approach each moment with openness to experience: referred to as a beginner's mind — approaching each sexual interlude as if it were the first.

All this requires is a little bit of practice. Don't jump ahead with your thoughts. Instead, just keep pace with the wonderful information you receive through your senses. Follow whatever erotic thoughts emerge, responding spontaneously and naturally to your partner's body and touch and voice without analysing. Teach your mind to follow your fingertips and hand in discovering new sensations.

8. Share Your Favourite Sensations. Sexual energy increases for many of us when we can feel free to relate how we are feeling, right now, in the evolving experience of intimacy, and have our partner do the same. By describing sensations of closeness, we heighten feelings of sensuality. By using warm, sexually explicit conversation, complimenting how the other person looks and feels and expressing your own sensations of arousal and pleasure, you can more easily distance yourself from unwanted thoughts. If you're having trouble focusing or concentrating on lovemaking, learn to tell this to your partner and ask for warm, supportive help in releasing distractions.

9. Practice Strengthening Your Sex Muscles. To get the most out of sex, at every age, you need to be in great shape for it — in mind and body. 'Two powerful aphrodisiacs are a vigorous and well-cared for body and a lively personality,' write Robert N. Butler, MD, of Mount Sinai Medical Centre in New York, and Myrna I. Lewis, PhD. 'Much can be done to preserve the functioning of both.'

In one recent nine-month study of 95 previously inactive but healthy men (average age 48), researchers found that those who engaged in regular moderate to vigorous exercise reported up to a 30 percent increase in frequency of intercourse, with a 25 percent increase in the frequency of orgasms. They also reported increases in other arousal measures, such as passionate kissing and caressing. In contrast, the control subjects, who didn't exercise, experienced no improvements and actually saw slight decreases in their sexual frequency. Here are two sensible suggestions to improve your sexual relationship.

* Stay physically fit. Regular exercise has been linked to heightened sensuality and sexuality.
* Do the PC exercise regularly (this is another Tantric favourite). Beyond a balanced approach to everyday physical activity, there's a valuable exercise that takes just a few seconds and can be done almost anywhere at any time, by both men and women, to strengthen the sex-related sphincter muscles of the pelvic floor and, at least in some cases, help improve sexual responsiveness.

It's called the Kegel (KAY-GILL) exercise, named after Arnold H. Kegel, MD, the physician who re-discovered (I say 're-discovered' for it was long known to the Tantric masters in India and even described in their journals) and developed it in the late 1940s and early 1950s. In both men and women, the pubococygeus (PC) muscle tends to progressively atrophy from disuse through our lives.

Studies report that, compared with women who have strong well-toned PCs, women with weak PCs — and this includes many and perhaps most women over age 45 — are more frequently troubled with incontinence (involuntary urination) and are more often sexually dissatisfied. Weak PCs in men may contribute to incontinence, inability to achieve and maintain an erection, poor ejaculatory control and perhaps even problems related to the seminal vesicles and prostrate gland.

PC exercises have enabled some women to climax more readily and intensely, and the exercises may even assist men to achieve easier erections and more control of orgasm.

To become toned, the PC must be exercised regularly. Dr Kegel found that to learn the sensation of the PC contracting, you can start by interrupting urination. He recommended that to help the PC do most of the work itself, you should at first leave it relaxed when urinating and, once the flow has begun, make an effort to stop it, let it start again, stop it, and so on. After a few trials, most people can consciously tense the PC by simple mental command, anytime and anywhere, and then should use the occasional interruption of urination only as a simple check.

Practice doing the PC exercise a number of times during the day. However, there is some evidence to suggest that performing it upon first awakening and before urinating, while the bladder is very full, may not be beneficial. Any other time is fine. Tense the PC strongly, hold for one or two seconds. Relax for several seconds. Repeat this cycle so that you complete five to ten contractions in a set. You might also include quick flexing and relaxing sequences. As you gain strength and control, progressively increase the intensity of the PC exercise contractions, holding some for more than the usual one or two seconds. At first, the muscles may fatigue quickly. Don't overdo it. For many of us, 60 to 100, one-second to five-second contractions performed inconspicuously through the day is a reasonable goal.

10. Share Sexual 'Pillow Talks' with Your Partner. Sex is intensely personal. We all feel vulnerable about it. Some of us may be able to have a satisfying love life without talking about it, but that's very rare, especially in long-term relationships. In a study of 805 nurses, women with multiple orgasms did not get them by accident. They identified what they liked, chose sensual/sexual touches and pacing that gave them maximum pleasure and communicated to their partners what aroused them most.

It turns out that many of the most common sexual difficulties can be eased or overcome with open, sensitive, ongoing 'pillow talk'— an intimate sexual conversation with your partner.

Acknowledge your awkwardness or anxiety. When you begin a discussion on sex with your loved one, says Dr Alperstein. 'Acknowledge your fears. Be specific. Don't say, "I want more affection". Say, "I want you to hug me and give me a special kiss when we first get together after work. I want to hold your hand when we go for a walk or sit by side. And I want to be held for a little while each night without that always being interpreted as a sexual invitation." '

Have sexual heart talks. Consider taking turns sharing your innermost feelings and thoughts. Be careful not to interrupt, and give your undivided attention. Be specific, caring, open and honest:

Create a wish list. Over a week or two, you and your partner write down everything you wish the other would do for you sexually, from more cuddling, hugs and kisses to affectionate notes to specific intimate caresses. Next, rank your wishes in order from easiest-to-ask-for to the most difficult. Then, once or twice a month, you each reveal the easiest items on your lists and eventually work your way down to the more difficult requests.

One ground rule to follow: You both have the right to say no whenever you are uncomfortable with a request.

For most people, the sexual wishes that are easiest to request are also easiest to grant. Typically, they have to do with expressions of affection out of bed; hugs, kisses and light caresses in everyday situations. The combination of asking for affection and getting it can have a surprisingly positive impact on the relationship as a whole.

The Power of Touch

As you're holding this book in this moment, what are you experiencing with your sense of touch? Observe what your fingers and hands are feeling. Are your fingertips touching the binding of the book or the jacket? Is the binding smooth or rough? Is the book cover sleek and slippery, printed on coated paper? Are the four fingers of each hand holding the book open while your thumbs rest on the page you are now reading? Is the paper pleasurable to your touch? Does it feel soft or harsh? Run your fingertips lightly up and down the page. Is it possible to feel any slight bumps or indentations of the ink? Flip the pages with your thumb. Is it pleasurable for you to sense the pages rapidly slipping away from under your thumb?

Perhaps the book feels heavy on your fingers and is setting up muscle tension in your fingers and thumbs, pressure on the palms of your hands? You may be reading this book while you are riding a bus to work on a freezing-cold morning. Or it may be summer and you are lying on a hammock beside a swimming pool.

Or you may be feeling lonely, longing to be cuddled in someone's arms, yearning for the warmth and heartbeat and solace of another human body. Poet-composer Rod McKuen says, 'The need to touch someone can be so great at times that it's as close to madness as I ever hope to come.'

Touch is the most important, and yet the most neglected, of our senses.

We can survive without sight as blind people do. We can survive without hearing as deaf people do. We can survive without our sense of smell; smell is the first of our senses to leave us when we fall asleep and the last to return when we awaken — that's why people often cannot smell a fire when they are asleep. Our ancient ancestors and the earliest of humans, walking on all fours, had their noses close to the ground to sniff the odours that alerted them to danger. Now, as we climb up the evolutionary ladder, our sense of smell is slowly dying. But we cannot survive and live with any degree of comfort and mental health when we are not able to feel. A complete loss of our sense of touch can send us into mental and emotional imbalance and even lead to psychotic break down.

A study of boredom was done at McGill University in the United States in which male subjects lay on beds in lighted cubicles 24 hours a day. They wore translucent plastic visors that permitted light to reach their eyes, but the objects they saw were blurred. They lay with their heads on U-shaped pillows that limited but did not cut off their ability to hear. On their hands they wore cotton gloves and cardboard cuffs extending beyond their fingertips so that at no time were they able to feel anything with their fingers and hands. In a short time — only a matter of hours for some — they were unable to think clearly. Their thoughts became disjointed and incoherent. They thought in fragments of sentences, and then forgot in the middle of a sentence what they were thinking. They experienced numbness, lethargy, a free-floating sensation of their physical beings gradually disintegrating.

At birth, we derive all sensations and information through the largest sensory organ of our bodies — our skin. The tactile sensations that we receive when we are snuggled up to a warm body, feeling the rhythm of a beating heart as we suckle at a breast or drink from a bottle are vital to our survival. They set up electrical impulses that travel along our neural pathways and help create biochemical reactions that enable our brains to develop and function.

Many of us, however, go through life touch-starved. We suffer malnutrition of the senses and rarely experience that wonderful feeling of having our touch hunger fully satisfied. Skin hunger is an apt analogy. Each of us is a combination of many of the 106 chemical elements currently recognized by science. These elements are contained in the chemicals produced in our brains. Touch stimulates the production of chemicals in the brain, and these feed our blood, muscle, tissue, nerve calls, glands, hormones and organs. Deprived of touch to stimulate these chemicals, we may be as starved as if we were deprived of food.

It is ironic that our society, which is uncomfortable with touch and usually does not encourage it, certainly encourages it when it serves the creation of profit. Underneath many commercials on television and advertisements in magazines is an appeal to our sense of pleasure through touch. Toilet tissue commercials talk about how 'soft, softer and softest' they are. A man's cheek is more pleasant to touch when he uses a particular brand of shaving cream or lotion. Hair is smoother to touch when it is washed with the advertiser's product. But let people talk about touching for humanitarian reasons — just to enhance understanding and good feelings between people — and we consider them bizarre, strange or oversexed.

We talk about but do not act out on our need for touch. Listen to these common expressions:

> Of a sentimental or emotional occasion we say, 'It was a touching experience.'
>
> We tell an inspiring speaker, 'Your talk touched me deeply.'
>
> 'Don't be so touchy,' we tell a grouchy person. (In fact, if a grouch were a touchy person — touching others or being touched — he undoubtedly would be less grouchy.)
>
> One of the most frequently spoken sentences in the world is probably 'Let's keep in touch,' said as we part from a friend, relative, colleague, or acquaintance. How much less alienated we would be if, instead of just mouthing that phrase, we did actually touch.
>
> Touch is also the most social of our senses. We can see, taste, smell and hear by and for ourselves, but touch is the one sense requiring us to interact with others — at least most of the time. Literally, to reach out and touch someone. In a higher sense, touch gives us all belonging.

There is something godlike about the power every one of us possesses in our hands and fingers to brings pleasure and give meaning to another human being. We can all be creators of well-being, for ourselves and for other.

Why do we have a sense of touch at all? What is the intention of existence in giving us millions of sense receptors throughout our bodies and embedded in our skin? Nature is our greatest protector. Above all else, our sense of touch alerts us to danger — through temperature, vibration and pressure. Nature wants the human race to always be protected and grow.

Your fingers or hands touch a hot stove, and without thinking, your reflexes draw you away from danger. Put your hand into a bucket of ice and you will also draw your hand away in an involuntary action to escape the pain. Your sense receptors find these extreme temperatures unsafe for survival. You go to climb a ladder and as you put hands on its two sides, delicate vibrations tell your sense receptors that it is dangerously shaky.

You're driving your car and you need to suddenly apply the brakes. Instantly you feel nuances of vibration on the sole of your foot, warning you that your brakes are not holding with their customary tightness.

Among Nature's intentions in giving us touch is to inform and educate us, to help us differentiate surfaces and motions. Run your fingertips lightly across surfaces near you right now. Your sense of touch is capable of discriminating between a smooth pane of glass and etched glass; between sandpaper and slick paper; between a porcelain plate and a paper plate.

There are 1,300 nerve endings per square inch in your fingertips. You don't even have to touch with your whole fingertip; you often get information by touching just with your fingernail. We can get information from locations a sixteenth of an inch apart on our skin. That's why, if you are lying on your stomach on the beach, you can feel that an insect is crawling on you, or a fly has landed on you.

Touch is so efficient that even different degrees of pressure inform us. Deep pressure stimulates different nerve endings than does light pressure. An airy touch often says something affectionate, nurturing or sexual. A heavy touch to the same part of the body may be a warning.

Nature is not only our guard and teacher; it is also a wily seductress. The same receptors that alert and educate us also lure us into sex. Delicate play over our bodies transmits delicious messages from our skin to our brains to our sexual organs.

The most exquisite pleasure the human brain knows comes through sexual orgasm. This shows what an efficient creator nature is as she says, in effect, 'I'll give you your greatest pleasure; you give me the greatest number of humans.' To ensure our constant attraction to sex, Nature has made the most sensitive areas of our bodies, next to our fingertips, lips and tongues, the clitoris and the penis.

About a third of our five million receptors are in our hands, the most sensitive receptors being concentrated in our palms and fingertips. To test how highly sensitive your fingertips and palms are, put this book down for a moment. Lightly stroke the fingertips of one hand against the fingertips of the other hand. You may feel a pleasurable stirring in your genital area, perhaps a tickling sensation, perhaps a feeling of well-being. Your mood may become lighter and more joyful; your body may feel relaxed. Now stroke the palm of one hand with the index finger of the other. Continue doing so for a few moments; you may find yourself gasping, with the eroticism of that simple touch.

The next-most-sensitive areas are our lips and tongues. To test your lips' sensitivity, pluck a hair from your head. Pull it back and forth across your upper and lower lips. The receptors on your tongue are so exquisitely attuned that the fine hair, infinitesimal in its circumference, can feel like twine. A particle of food caught between your teeth can feel like a stone, and your tongue keeps trying to clean it out.

When our sense receptors receive the stimuli of touch, what happens within our body? The touch sparks a minor volt of electricity that shoots into a neuron. We have a hundred billion neurons, or nerve cells. Each is separated from every other one by a junction called a synapse, As our electrical charge goes through a neuron, it stimulates a chemical neurotransmitter, which sparks across that synapse and ignites another electrical impulse through the next neuron, which does the same for the next neuron, and so on. Our touch or someone's touch on you is the lever that gives the message. Your brain is the receiver.

Your brain receives the message in its pleasure centre if you are being enjoyably caressed, embraced or stroked. It receives the message in a pain centre if you stub your toe or accidentally bite your tongue. Our tongues hurt so much when we accidentally bite them, because they have some of our most sensitive receptors. Our brain also receives the message in its executive, fact-absorbing or fact-analysing, part that tells us the texture, temperature and shape of what we are feeling — whether it is rough or smooth, hard or soft, cold or hot, a light pat or a hard pressure, whether an object is curved, pointed, round, rectangular, flat or cube-shaped.

In expressing loving feelings, a touch says more than words do. Let's say you are with your lover. The two of you see something that delights you. You take each other's hand and give secret squeezing signals that say, 'I'm sharing this with you, my love. This is something the two of us have together that nobody else is part of.'

When lovers quarrel, their first action toward reconciliation is frequently a touch. The warmth and pressure of their skin starts healing their wounds before conversation does.

Our bodies digest the loving meaning from such touch as if it were health-giving food. It is likely that the constant 'up' feeling, the high when we're in love, is the result of having a steady supply of tender squeeze and touch signals. It is the absence of skin talk that makes our lives so barren when we are without love.

When I counsel couples, I ask if they feel loved by each other. I am not surprised when a wife says, 'No, I don't really feel loved by my husband.' Frequently he is astonished, and he exclaims, 'But I often tell you I love you.'

Saying 'I love you' is a combination of sounds spoken into the air. Touching loved ones records your emotions on their bodies; they feel your love. A wife says that she gets weak-kneed with joy when her husband, helping her with her coat, squeezes her shoulder. Another woman told a researcher, 'I would rather be held by my husband every day — though not 24 hours a day — than have a Cadillac convertible.'

Desmond Morris who is considered an expert on humanology, says, 'A single intimate body contact will do more than all the beautiful words in the dictionary. The ability that physical feelings have to transmit emotional feelings is truly astonishing.'

Obviously, when you combine the power of touch with the power of words, you make your message all the stronger. I will take you through some powerful touch-techniques in the next chapter. For now, read on.

Love is the most celebrated of emotions. This we all instinctively understand and accept. Yet it is largely a mystery; looked for and longed for. And for most, lasting love is rarely found. The result is disappointment, and worse, bitterness and a sense of betrayal, cynicism and disillusionment.

Love and intimacy is an emotional process that takes time and care. It is largely a matter of ideas and choices in daily living. Love is neither fleeting nor purely romantic. It is not based on novelty or restricted to youth.

In fact, from a deeper perspective, to a great extent the passion in your love defines the way you live.

The emotion of love emerges from the self but is based, first of all, in caring for another person as you care for yourself. If you can come to better understand what love is and refuse to suffocate it or take it for granted, then love becomes an invigorating force that reaches into the future and sets a foundation for trust and excitement, for sharing whole-heartedly with someone for a truly meaningful life.

Researchers all over the world have confirmed two central truths: First, that loving relationships are built, not found. And second, they have little, if anything, to do with luck. Below are some practical ways you can create the relationship of your dreams.

Secrets of Creating a Passionate Relationship with your Partner

1. Take Time at the End of the Day to Harmonize with Your Partner. There's no denying it: research from all over the world has found that intimate relations are tied to a variety of biological forces. And researchers have also discovered a key relationship between sexual energy and the natural, ongoing influence of two biological cycles — the 24-hour circadian rhythm and the 60- to 90-minute ultradian rhythms. Successful, sexually satisfied couples tend to have overall activity patterns, appetite, need for diversion and sexual rhythms 'all occurring in harmony.' In contrast, unsynchronized sexual energy cycles produce some of the most frustrating sexual problems: When one of you is sexually aroused and sensually energetic, the other one isn't, or when one of you is in the mood for comforting, nonsexual cuddling, the other desires exciting, active sex.

The more you can align your daily energy cycles with those of your partner, the greater your chances for lifelong, mutually satisfying intimacy — the best of what sex can and should be. Couples with exceptionally intimate and lasting sexual relationships tend to unconsciously integrate their own individual ultradian and circadian rhythms. Research has also shown that couples complaining of lost sexual energy and unhappiness frequently report conflict and imbalance across these areas.

Years ago, at the end of the day in almost any town or village in Asia, America or Europe, you could see couples sitting together in rocking chairs or on a porch swing, gazing at the sunset, talking to each other, reflecting on the day. Without realizing it, these couples were synchronizing their circadian and ultradian rhythms and increasing their sexual energy. The shared quiet time and rocking rhythm helped to lower their stress levels and reduced the odds that tensions or frustrations would be passed on from one mate to the other.

Today, more and more couples rush home, hurry to prepare dinner, flip through the newspaper, eat quickly and then either collapse for the evening in front of the television or plunge into another round of scheduled activities. What's missing is a transition period — 15 or 20 minutes will do — to unplug from the stress and commotion and sit together quietly, without the television playing in the background, to tune into each other's energy rhythms and recover together from the day's pace.

Here are some ways couples can adopt to increase sexual harmony between themselves:

* Kissing and greeting each other whenever leaving and arriving, thereby using the sensory power of touch to help align your energy cycles.
* Slowing down the pace of the main meal and enjoying each other's dining companionship.
* Going for a shared early-morning or evening stroll.
* Spending time together fixing plans, deciding on the day ahead, or just pottering around the lawn or garden.

* Sitting together quietly, listening to music both enjoy and sipping a cup of tea or a glass of wine.
* Sharing a warm bath or gentle, rhythmic massage for 15 to 20 minutes prior to sexual intimacy.
* Stretching out on the sofa and holding each other — fully clothed, with nothing unhooked or unzipped — in a 'spoon' position, with one person wrapping arms around the other from behind. The warmth and comfort of this sensual embrace strengthens the closeness between each other and helps release stress.

In each of these simple actions, powerful verbal and nonverbal cues will help to synchronize your energy rhythms and renew and increase intimate bonds with your partner after time apart. In addition, the mind/body connection of gentle touching can also serve as subtle aphrodisiacs.

2. Enjoy Time for Humour. Every love relationship has its own unique reservoir of humour: private jokes and shared laughter, ticklish spots on the body, comic faces or favourite funny experiences together. Make it a point to find more moments to ignite this humour each day, to remember some of the comical situations you witnessed, or created, during the day. Usually there are lots of humorous little events and situations. Share these with each other.

As Erich Fromm states in the classic book *The Art of Loving*, 'Most people see the problem of love primarily as that of being loved, rather than of loving or of one's capacity to love.' And clearly a part of that capacity to love comes from cultivating your ability to share laughter, to be a loving person with a sense of fun, of play, of humour.

3. Make Time to Relax Together. The experience of love takes time — time to relate to each other. Perhaps even more important, the experience of love is also tied to the experience of time, a deepening sense of being together, of sharing experiences together, weaving these events and memories into a narrative, a love story, moving through time.

The intimacy and romance of love requires a biological bond as much as an emotional connection. To set the stage for a warmer bond with your loved one, spend a few key minutes when you greet your partner each morning and evening to hug, hold hands and kiss, thereby using touch to help synchronize your ultradian rhythms.

Instead of rushing through dinner and then plopping in front of the television, block out a few minutes to go for a walk, hand in hand, or sit side by side listening to music you both love, or take pleasure in some other activity together — such as gardening, enjoying a glass of wine or giving each other a back rub.

These kinds of shared daily experiences provide significant verbal and nonverbal cues that help renew intimate bonds after a day apart. As simple as they seem, they're vital to keeping the closeness and passion in your relationship.

4. Learn to Listen Well — It's Essential to Intimacy. Friendship is one of the under-appreciated foundations of love. Indeed, the bonds of friendship are essential to make love last. Without it love will falter. Friendship encompasses loyalty, trusting, caring, inspiring, sharing and wishing the other person well. And, not surprisingly, it adds a vital sense of meaning to sexual desire and satisfaction.

One of the reasons that love fades is neglect, and one of the principal kinds of neglect is the inability to listen well. In truth, in many cases the number one way a man may succeed in fulfiling woman's primary love needs is through communication.

'By learning to listen to a woman's feelings,' explains John Gray, author of *Men Are from Mars, Women Are from Venus*, 'a man can effectively shower a woman with caring, understanding, respect, devotion, validation and reassurance... Just as men need to learn the art of listening to fulfil a woman's primary love needs, women need to learn the art of empowerment. When a woman asks for the support of a man, she empowers him to be all that he can be. A man feels empowered when he is trusted, accepted, appreciated, admired, approved of and encouraged. The secret of empowering a man is never to try to change him or improve him... when you try to change him or improve him, he feels controlled, manipulated, rejected and unloved... And she mistakenly thinks he is not willing to change, probably because he does not love her enough.'

5. Share a Five Minute Snuggle (At Least Once a Day). Of all the ways in which people need each other, touching and holding is the most primary, the least evident and the hardest to describe.

'Holding contains the invisible threads that tie us to our existence,' says Ruthellen Josselson, PhD. 'From the first moments of our life to the last, we need to be held — or we fall. There are physical and emotional aspects of holding. The holding function of relationship not only provides care and meaning, it also provides hope.'

So make a point to loosen up a bit and spend time just holding your partner in a caring but non-sexual way.

6. Look into Each Other's Eyes. It should be clear that caring about each other — in virtually every imaginable way — is a central bond of identity in love. To help someone else grow can sometimes be the most difficult kind of caring, but it truly matters to love.

One of the most important ways we affirm our connection to loved ones is eye-to-eye. No matter how old you become, you never cease to need unconditional valuing in another's eyes — and in your own eyes. 'These looks are far beyond words,' says Dr Josselson. 'Eyes speak more profoundly than language of words. They express, surely and absolutely, how much and in what way we matter to the other. Words may lie; eyes cannot.'

In short, saying, 'I love you' in words pales in contrast to the potential power of expressing 'I love you' without any words, eye-to-eye.

7. Validate Your Over to Make it Stronger. For many of us, one of the best relationship advices would be to worry a bit less about what we think is important — money problems, career track, the annual vacation — and pay more attention to the little things. Begin with the power of validation.

'Letting your spouse/partner know in so many little ways that you understand him or her is one of the most powerful tools for healing your relationship,' explains John M. Gottman, PhD. 'Validation is simply putting yourself in your partner's shoes and imagining his or her emotional state. It's then a simple matter to let your mate know that you understand those feelings and consider them valid, even if you don't share them. Validation is an amazingly effective technique. It's as if you opened a door to welcome your partner.'

Validations (which often take as little as five seconds) can lead to genuine empathy and understanding between partners. Few things make a person feel more valued and loved. You can increase your empathy in many ways, such as acknowledging responsibility: 'Yes, I know this upsets you.' It feels like I really made you angry, didn't I? Or apologizing: 'I'm sorry. I was wrong.' Or expressing compliments by honestly praising your partner, and saying that you really admire something specific about him or her (this can have a remarkably positive effect on the rest of the conversation).

8. Express Appreciation to Increase Intimacy. Once you're making progress with validation, take a look at the power of appreciation. How many times has your day been brightened by one small, unexpected gesture of appreciation or caring? Unfortunately, many men think they score points with their partner when they do big things — like buying a car, replacing the refrigerator, setting up a new stereo or taking the family on a vacation. At the same time, many men assume that little things — opening doors, sharing loving glances, giving hugs or kisses, saying 'I love you', sitting close together when watching a movie or television, checking with each other first before making plans, holding hands, saying 'you look great', buying flowers or writing thank-you notes — count very little when compared to the big things. But there is evidence of many women keeping track of every gesture done. No matter how big or small a gift of love or caring is, it scores a point.

9. Tell Your Partner Why you Appreciate Him/Her. Here's another love-building exercise: Arrange for five minutes in private to tell your partner many of the specific reasons why you appreciate him or her. What meaning and inspiration can you and your spouse find in the detailed history of your relationship? Make a list ahead of time so you can 'bathe' your loved one in appreciation. Here are some suggestions: What attracted you to your lover in the first place? What specific qualities about him or her do you admire the most? What were some of the highlights and moments of laughter and fun when you first began dating? What made the relationship worth pursuing? How did your partner help the two of you overcome any differences or obstacles along the way? What are your favourite memories of your first year in the relationship? What efforts by your partner have helped the relationship make it through the difficult times? Once you've made a list of specific experiences and qualities that you appreciate in your loved one, share it with your loved one.

One rule is to be followed to make this practice effective: The partner who is listening must not make judgements or negate any of the appreciative comments ('I'm not really that considerate...' 'I never looked that sexy; besides, now I've got to lose ten kilos...'). Then find another time to exchange roles and give your spouse five minutes to express some of the specific things she or he appreciates about you.

This simple exercise helps you stop taking each other for granted and can effectively reawaken an awareness of the qualities in your partner — and yourself — that form the shared, sometimes hidden, foundation of your love.

10. Give Importance and Attention to Sexual Intimacy. It is necessary that both partners give their time, attention and importance to being committed to a proactive sexual relationship. Research has shown that couples who enjoy life-long intimacy and good communication treat their sexual relationship on a high priority and are willing to do whatever it takes to keep it alive, vibrant and satisfying. Sex is an important part of a fulfiling relationship between a man and a woman.

Tantric Meditation 2

The Hollow Bamboo

The essence of Tantra is receptivity to energy. As individuals we have access to very small amounts of energy, but when we become empty inside and open ourselves to receive from nature, from the divine, we can become a vessel or channel for unlimited energy.

The meditation is simple, yet powerful. It was a special method recommended by Tilopa, a great Tantric master for his disciple Naropa. It reflects a spiritual reality: when we connect within ourselves we discover that we are hollow inside; there is a core of emptiness, or inner space. Being like a hollow bamboo helps us to get in touch with this reality. The meditation is done standing. You should feel relaxed and comfortable.

- Breathe normally, close your eyes, and let the tip of your tongue touch the roof of your mouth. This helps to create an energy circuit within your body. Imagine that you are a hollow bamboo, a hollow, empty vessel: receptive, passive.
- You may experience a gentle swaying, like a bamboo being caressed by a breeze. The strength of the bamboo lies in its flexibility; it can withstand the strongest storm because it can bend with the wind. Feel this flexibility in yourself as you sway and bend.
- Relax into this experience. You are not to do anything more than this. You are not to expect anything. Everything is perfect the way it is. Many different things can happen with this meditation. You may feel energy begin to pour through you like a waterfall. You may feel that your boundaries are disappearing and your inner

hollowness is merging with a greater emptiness surrounding you. Or you may simply feel empty and silent inside. Whatever you experience, let everything be okay the way it is. This meditation can also be done with a partner.

* Begin with each partner standing alone, becoming a hollow bamboo.
* Then after 10-15 minutes, one partner remains a bamboo while the other becomes a gentle breeze.
* Breeze: Make the sounds of a wind blowing through a bamboo grove. Move freely around the room, gently touching or pushing the bamboo from different sides.
* Bamboo: Sway with the breeze as it blows against you, Enjoy being a bamboo, responding to the breeze. It is so simple and easy.
* Continue in this way for about 15 minutes, and then change roles. The hollow bamboo can also be a beautiful meditation to do outdoors, especially in a forest, or where there is an open space with a strong wind blowing.

Advanced Tantric Meditation 2

Stop!

Many people are familiar with a meditation method used by George Gurdjieff, the eccentric mystic, called the 'Stop Exercise'. In the middle of some activity, such as dancing, Gurdjieff would suddenly say to his disciples, 'Stop!' And everyone would freeze, becoming completely still and motionless. Few people know that this technique is much more ancient and is described by Lord Shiva in *Vigyan Bhairav* Tantra: 'Just as you have the impulse to do something, stop'. When you suddenly stop a gap happens, because the body and mind are engaged in an activity that is interrupted. There is a moment of disconnection, separation. It takes you out of any automatic pattern or habit, and brings you strongly into the present moment.

You can explore this with your beloved, while making love, and this can be a playful and profound experience for both of you. Agree, before entering into lovemaking, that either of you can say 'stop!' at any moment. Let the pause happen for a few seconds, until the same person starts to move again. Perhaps you don't want to try this at the height of your orgasm as you might have passed the point of no return!

You will be surprised how much awareness and sensitivity this simple method can create for both of you. When you suddenly stop, the energy that was involved in the outer activity of sex will move inward, bringing you both deeper, to the core of your being. It can also provoke a negative reaction, as the mind tends to cling to its ideas about goal-orientation and 'doing'. If this happens, you can be certain that the mind is your master and not you. Take a deep breath, relax and continue with the meditation. You can also try this technique alone, in many different areas of your life.

For example, when you are walking quickly to work in the morning, already thinking of the day ahead, what has to be done at the office, suddenly say to yourself 'stop'. Just stop. Don't move. Never mind what other people might think. Remain motionless for a few seconds, feeling how the momentum of life carries you in a certain direction and you are suddenly disconnected, thrown back to your own centre.

3

Touch

'Being is the eternal ever-present I AM. Just Be. Being is not mind. You need a shift of consciousness from mind to Being.'

Advice from a Tantric Master

Tantra says we can celebrate life when the idea of separation, or dualism, disappears and allows people to meet on all levels of consciousness — physical, intellectual, emotional and spiritual.

While most fundamentalist religions focus on the elimination of sensual pleasures, Tantra welcomes the full expression of bodily pleasure, recognizing that in the body is hidden the 'bodiless' or the spiritual.

If you can learn to be conscious of the body, you can be conscious of the Universe.

What Buddha said in his teachings on self-awareness can also be said of Tantra, 'The truth of the Universe can only be realized within the framework of the physical body'.

We create our own reality, and it can be anything we want it to be.

It's possible to study Tantra for years, learning techniques, meditations, and the many nuances of the Tantric lifestyle, but Tantra assumes you already are what you will become, and enlightenment is already yours — all you need to do is realize it.

It is like sitting in a dark room when all you have to do is turn on the light.

Tantra doesn't ask you to believe anything. In fact, it says let go of all belief systems.

My Master would say to me, 'You are separated from Being, the inner you, because your mind, and your identification with the outer you — the illusionary you — demands all your attention like a baby or a little child, and requires all your energy to satisfy it. It robs you of consciousness, and strengthens the illusion that you are no more than a physical form with material needs and wants because your self, the ego, is identified with it. You haven't yet learned how to appreciate the physical body, even love it, without the self, the ego, or being identified with it.

'An ordinary artist may be identified with his or her work, a great artist is not — he or she is detached. Love your body, but it's not you. Appreciate, and use your mind, but it's not you. Experience, and enjoy, your emotions, but they're not you. Don't identify with them. Your body, mind, and emotions, are tools, or one tool, as are events and situations, for one purpose — to help you attain enlightenment, and liberation from illusion.

'Every molecule, every atom, in your physical body and everything else from a stone to a star, has this life-energy else the molecules and atoms would have no cohesion and they, and the object, would fly apart. This life-energy creates a single energy-field within and around the object, which is vibrant and has consciousness. You are not a physical body with a spirit — you are spirit with a physical body.

'The purpose of a physical body is not only to make money, acquire power, or gain fame, or even happiness. If that is all it is, and even if you get them, it will be all for nothing because, in the end, you will die and leave everything behind. The purpose of your life, why you have a physical body, is to experience every step, to be conscious of this moment, for each step has within it every step — the first and the last and all the steps between — and this one step is enlightenment, and your whole life, is enfolded in this present moment.

'Ultimately, enlightenment is found through the physical body, not out of it, or else there would be no purpose in having it or through an event or situation; else there would be no point in it happening. What you perceive as your physical body, subject to disease, old age, infirmity, and finally death, is simply a distorted reflection in the mirror of pure consciousness. The physical body is illusionary but behind the illusion of mortality and disintegration is immortality and incorruptibility — it is the doorway to the divine.'

And so, he would conclude, 'Appreciate your physical body as you might appreciate a work of art, take care of it, love it, but don't identify with it. Use it as a tool for your enlightenment instead of for indulgence, greed, and self-enhancement. If you cannot find enlightenment through the physical body, you never will — for that is its purpose.'

> The modern day mystic, Osho, was once asked the question, 'Isn't Tantra a way of indulgence?' His answer will give you a clearer understanding of what the whole purpose of the Tantra path is. Osho replied, 'It is not. It is the only way to get out of indulgence. It is the only way to get out of sexuality. No other way has ever been helpful for man; all other ways have made man more and more sexual. Sex has not disappeared. The religions have made it only more poisoned. It is still there — in a poisoned form. Yes, guilt has arisen in man, but sex has not disappeared. It cannot disappear because it is a biological reality. It is existential; it cannot simply disappear by repressing it. It can disappear only when you become so alien that you can release the energy encapsulated in sexuality — not by repression is the energy released, but by understanding. And once the energy is released, out of the mud the lotus... the lotus has to come up out of the mud, it has to go higher, and repression takes it deeper into the mud. No, Tantra is not a way of indulgence. It is the only way of freedom.'

Tantra says: 'Whatsoever is has to be understood and through understanding changes occur of their own accord. Indulgence is suicidal

— as suicidal as repression. These are the two extremes that Buddha says to avoid. One extreme is repression, the other extreme is indulgence, Just be in the middle; neither be repressive, nor be indulgent. Just be in the middle, watchful, alert, and aware. It is your life! — it has to be understood.'

Sexual Touching

We long to be touched, and touched some more. The same cry runs through the words of many couples worldwide and it goes something like this. The husband says, 'My wife never makes an overture. If I didn't approach her, I think we'd go for years without sex. I'd like it if once in a while, while we're sitting watching television or reading, she'd reach over, unzip my pants, and fondle me. But she never makes a move to touch me.'

The wife says, 'My husband doesn't fondle me enough. He gets into sex too fast. I need more warming-up by being touched. I'm afraid to touch him because that automatically means sex to hem. I want to be caressed and held before sex.'

Underneath all these expressions of unhappiness is a plea for more gentle and prolonged tactile experience as part of the sex act. During the most intimate act we perform in our entire lives — making love — we deny each other the most gorgeous pleasure we will ever know, the light, soft, easy, slow motions of our hands and fingers. This is exactly the issue the ancient masters of the erotic techniques of Tantra were trying to address when they delved deeply into the study of the sexual nature of the human being.

After centuries in which pleasure was labelled as licentious and hedonistic, we are having a hard time adjusting to a new pro-pleasure ethic. We need to be given psychological and societal permissions to touch our bodies in ways designed to do nothing more than yield pleasure. Many couples, spending hours in bed in pursuit of pleasure, share uneasy, gnawing feelings that 'we really ought to be getting up and doing something worthwhile.'

Masters and Johnson originated a program of touch experiences known as Sensate Focus (it was more of a reframing rather than an invention in my opinion since this is simply a modification of one of the primary techniques of heightening your sense of touch-awareness practised in Tantra, and has been advised and used to great rewards for hundreds of years, much before Masters and Johnson came up with the idea). During this two-week program of Sensate Focus, couples are instructed to start out touching each other's body lovingly, slowly, tenderly, gently, playfully, everywhere but in the genital and breast areas, in the privacy of their rooms. They take turns, one being the giver the other the receiver. They are told that it is okay to receive erotic pleasure for themselves without feeling any need to reciprocate during their touch session.

Touch assignments show couples that when they feel exquisite pleasure and sensual stimulation without the burden of having to perform the sex act, they can repeatedly experience arousal and desire.

Over and over, an impotent male sees evidence of how, when the pressure to achieve penetration is removed, he is capable of achieving and maintaining erection. The non-orgasmic female learns how her body can respond with intense desire for orgasm when her face, lips, eyes, ears, abdomen, knees, shoulders and buttocks are stroked, and her clitoris, vagina and breasts, her most sexually sensitive areas, are deliberately left untouched.

From such touch, waves of joy and desire can surge through the body until one feels, in the words of one couple, 'like a penis or vagina crying out for genital contact,' throbbing with the need for release through orgasm. Eventually, in the two-week program, couples are given permission to engage in intercourse, having first learned how to touch each other.

Another noted team of researchers from the Centre for Marital and Sexual studies in Long Beach, California, USA, have designed other touch techniques:

* The Foot Caress in which couples bathe each other's feet and legs. Try this and you'll become aware of how soothing it is to

have loving hands fuss over you with soap and water. Sit on a chair with your feet in a pan of warm water while your partner sits on the floor in front of you. Close your eyes and experience the water being poured over your calves, ankles and feet, the creamy soap suds massaged up and down your legs.

* The Hair Caress in which couples gently wash, comb or brush each other's hair. It can be spine-tingling to feel the warm breeze from your lover's breathe tickling through your hair.
* Breathing Caress in which a couple lie closely, face to face or in the spoon position, one's back against the other's front, and synchronize their breathing. It becomes hypnotic to feel each other's rhythmic abdomens as you inhale and exhale.
* Body Imagery in which you stand nude in front of a three-way, full-length mirror and touch every part of yourself from the top of your head down to the soles of your feet, not skipping the belly-button or pubic hair. You say out loud what you like or dislike about that part of your body. After voicing these feelings, the small size of one's penis or of one's breasts may never again seem so important.

Most innovative of these touch exercises is the Sexological Examination in which couples are taught to lightly finger each others' genitals, pelvises and anuses to determine their spots of greatest sexual responsiveness. It's well know that the most sensitive area in the male is usually the corona, or crown of the penis, the shaft and base may have lesser sensitivity. The man is taught to put a well-lubricated, gentle finger inside the vagina and to move it clockwise from the top down the right side to the bottom and then back up the left side, as if the inside of the vagina were the face of a clock. He helps his partner identify her 'time zones' of greatest pleasure. Being touched at 'two' and 'four o' clock' may not do a thing for her, while being touched at 'six' and 'eight o'clock' may transport her into ecstasy.

An aspect of sexual touch that often leads to misunderstandings is the timing of it. A sudden touch makes us undergo the startle reflex, a reflex we are born with. Our startled bodies may perceive such a touch not as enjoyable but as threatening. Your lover puts his moist tongue into your ear and you reflexively jump. He mistakenly thinks that you don't enjoy this sex play. You do enjoy it — but only after you've reached a state of arousal. You and your lover start foreplay when he suddenly starts going down on you for oral sex. But you need more fondling first, so you hold him back by pressing your hand on his shoulder. He misinterprets your touch message as meaning that you don't want oral sex. You do, but not yet. Some men make sexual overtures that are just the opposite of what the sense receptors of their partners crave. They give an 'affectionate' smack to a woman's bottom or they grab her breasts from behind. They don't understand why they get an angry response instead of an amorous one because of the startle effect.

The pace and pressure of our fingers is also important to good sex. Early in the act we enjoy a feather massage, long, slow strokes with airy pressure. Only after we are aroused do we want short, rapid, intense strokes with heavier pressure. A partner whose finger probes prematurely with short, hard motions can literally turn off pleasurable sensations rising in us.

Strangely, the most used furniture for sex — the bed — is many times not the best place for it. Beds don't have built-in-armrests. An elderly gentleman told me that throughout his long, sexually active life he always preferred to make love on a sofa, because the back provided a base from which he could thrust harder. 'In bed,' he explained, 'your body is moving in empty space, on a sofa you have the back to give you leverage.'

Not only the furniture on which sex takes place, but the location can be stimulating. Some lovers like the excitement of being in a semi-public situation to see how much they can get away with in public. In counselling, men have said that they like to have their genitals fondled by a spouse or lover while driving a car, enjoying the sensation of the penis hardening in their clothes. They get a special erotic thrill by risking being seen by people in other cars.

My partner and I often sit on the same side of booths in restaurants (waiters are startled when we do that because it seems that long term couples just don't sit next to each other) so we can gently touch while dining or she can rest her head on my shoulder while waiting for food to arrive. It also allows us to hold hands, something that's probably the most fulfiling and comforting act if done with full awareness. If we're feeling especially playful we might actually kiss and hug each other while we wait. This play doesn't necessarily mean we're feeling sexy, it is just one more way to be affectionate regardless of whether we are in public or not.

An exciting part of semi-public sexual touching is that it happens when we're clothed. Being touched through clothes can sometimes stimulate more than being touched in the customary way and place, naked in bed. Such a repetitive start to sex becomes downright boring. Being lightly and delicately touched through our clothes introduces a variety of stimuli that our physiology craves. Clothing can provide pleasurable friction. With clothes, without clothes, in private, in public, it's important to understand that it is more the pressure, pace, temperature and vibrations of our touch, and less the shape, size, style or gender of our genitals that creates the ecstasy we seek.

Regardless of our age, we all have the desire at some time to feel nurtured by another, a pull to return to the conditions of infancy. Even if it is only for a few moments, we need to recapture the sensations of being taken care of and protected by someone else, of not needing to do for ourselves. For those few moments when we are encircled by another's arms we can stop being our own doers and providers. We enjoy a respite from the intense pressures of living. We enter into a higher realm of consciousness — are lifted above the ordinary plane of living. The feel of a sincere loving embrace can do that for us.

Every one of us has sexual perception as unique as our fingerprints. No two people have sense receptors that respond exactly the same way to touch. This is why a man who thinks he is a great lover and becomes annoyed when a partner tries to tell him how she likes to be touched, may actually be a poor lover. Lovemaking is best when two people teach each other as they share, with their touch, what their areas of greatest pleasure are. **Our most effective sex organs are not our genitals but our minds.**

During my research for this book, I asked many men and women questions regarding their sex lives, and what they felt could be improved, altered or changed about them. The answers were extremely revealing in their honesty and I have incorporated many of the concerns and given solutions to them within this book.

Here is the view of a beautiful, single woman, 42-years-old, and full of the passion of life, who is searching for the true relationship of her life. I share it with my male readers so that they may better understand the perspective of many women out there, and become better lovers for it.

> *What is the difference between having sex and making love?*
>
> Honestly, I don't know. Recently, I've realized that I've never actually been in love (even though I've been married twice). I imagine that making love would be more intense on many levels — physical, emotional and spiritual — than just having sex, which I suppose is purely physical.
>
> *Is the sexual experience different for women than it is for men, and if so, why and how?*
>
> I would guess so. From what I've heard and what I've read, men see the sex act as merely a physical/recreational act. Certainly, my own experience would bear that out. Women like to feel that there's an emotional connection between themselves and the person they are having sex with (I believe this is the same for homosexual and heterosexual women), and often they will fool themselves into believing that there is an emotional connection when there is none.
>
> In my experience, men often take a very primitive approach to sex — they want to sow their seed in an effort to ensure that their genes are carried on into the next generation. This is also why it takes a long time for men to come round to the notion of adopting.

What does a woman look for in a fulfiling expression of love?

Personally, I'm looking for the whole package: a man who respects and appreciates me on every level and who wants a partner, not a mother.

How does a woman identify with her sexual energy and is she able to use it?

I think women are taught to feel as though they should be ashamed of their sexual desires. We are told that men are the predators and we should fight them off for as long as we can and then finally give in. It simply isn't true, though. I love sex and I'm not ashamed of it. Not only do I love sex, I love to have good, regular sex. I've been sexually active for 15 years and have only found two men who seemed to enjoy sex as much and as often as I did in all those years.

While there are a few things that I wouldn't entertain thoughts of, I'm open to trying plenty of things in a sexual relationship — and I think that being in a relationship is the key to unlocking an unfettered approach to sexuality.

With someone on a one-night thingy, you're not going to go all out, that's just physical. You're fizzing with hormones, you spot a guy you like, you chat him up and take him home or go back to his place. In that sort of a situation, it's going to be very straightforward sex; you're just interested in the destination, not the journey. In a relationship, you're much more likely to play with each other. Sexy phone calls and emails when he's at work, slipping your panties off in the taxi on the way home and giving them to him, writing him erotic letters, treating him to a whole afternoon of him-focused foreplay, really finding out what pushes his buttons — and then pushing them! All of that and more.

Women need to admit that they love sex as much as men and give themselves permission to enjoy it. Maybe, as women get older, however, they lose their inhibitions and listen to what they are thinking and feeling and ask for — or take! — what they want. Hmmmmm, have I answered this question yet?

How important is sexual satisfaction to a woman's happiness? Can she be fulfiled if it is not present?

I think sexual satisfaction is vital to a woman's satisfaction with her relationship. It's not vital to her happiness in life, though. Personally, I'm not in a relationship, but I am happier than I've ever been. It's been a long time (nearly 12 months) since I had sex and maybe if I'm without it for a bit longer; my answer to this question might be different! I don't like to think I will never have sex again, but I don't ache for it like I did when I was married. Yes — you read that right; I missed sex more when I was married (and not getting any!) than I do now.

Is the physical being and expression of a woman linked to her emotional and intellectual being and expression as well?

I think so. I know that when I'm unhappy I put on weight. And when I put on weight, I get unhappier — until I stop, take stock of what I'm so unhappy about and fix it. Then the weight falls off and I feel better about myself. I feel like myself again and my confidence returns. Being comfortable in my skin increases my confidence, and — as all the magazines tell us — that makes a person attractive.

How are a woman's body and her sexual organs different from a man's? Her psychological perspective on this.

Well, apart from the obvious physical differences, women are slower burners than men. It takes us that bit longer to get aroused than men. Men say that when they are aroused, their penises are sensitive. Well, as a woman I can tell you that, when aroused, everything is sensitive. A touch or a stroke on any part of the body — sometimes, just a look or a few whispered words — is sensational.

Oh! And kissing. Kissing is seriously under-estimated. Kissing is wonderful and it's really hard to find a man who understands that. Just sitting and kissing for hours is fantastic. Hugging is great too — proper hugs, I mean, not just putting your arms around someone.

Why do men and women view the sexual act differently?

I think a lot of it is conditioning. Men are told that they are ever-ready, so they try to live up to that and feel emasculated if they don't feel like having sex, and women are told that they're not really supposed to like it, that it's a duty they should perform.

Since the early experience of our lives shapes our attitudes towards sex, it is essential to carefully examine and study the conditioning we may be already carrying within us, even unconsciously, at this point in time, and then let go of the ones that don't serve us in our journey towards freedom. This is essential if one wants to walk the path of Tantra.

Overcoming Some Sexual Myths

Being conditioned by the years of our life and the society around us, most of us have absorbed attitudes about sex that powerfully influence our behaviour in unconscious ways.

Unless we become aware of them, there is little chance of transforming the way we act in our sexual lives. Many myths abound about our sexual lives and energy. Let's look at a few of them now, and begin the process of freeing our mind from limiting thoughts.

I give you seven myths below that bind us and freedom from which will lead to a greater understanding of our own sexual power.

Myth 1 — Sex is For Procreation Only. According to the Orthodox Christian perspective, sex is only for creating children, not pleasure. As a result the inherent joy and feeling of being alive that sex can bring us is poisoned with guilt. Think for a minute how many times you will make love in your lifetime. A friend of mine spontaneously came up with the figure 7,000. But to create one child, you need to make love only once. So what are you going to do with the other 6,999 times? The role of spiritually aware sex is to take care of these other times, to shift the emphasis in lovemaking from procreation to ecstasy.

Myth 2 — Sex is Shameful. This condemning attitude stems from the Western religious tradition of separating the flesh from the spirit. Of course, the ancient eastern philosophies are totally the reverse of this belief system.

The Western religious view has long been that sex represents the libido, the instinctual drive that cannot be controlled by the will; hence, it is regarded as dangerous. Spiritually aware sex will teach you new ways of perceiving the erotic experience, ways in which sex is honoured as a celebration, an act of creation, an art.

Myth 3 — Sex is Natural, so Don't Interfere With It. It often has been observed that 'When you're hot, you're hot; when you're not, you're not.' The idea this saying expresses is: Don't interfere with the natural flow of your libido; just 'let it happen'. Nature knows best. Consequently, some people take the view that the introduction of any formal practice or discipline into the realm of sex might interfere with their spontaneity. The sexual urge as we experience it individually is not nearly as natural as it seems. It is continuously being influenced by cultural conditioning. We are products of our culture, not just politically or in terms of diet or sports, but sexually as well.

The expression of sexual energy is both natural and cultural. Much of sex is simply a set of learned responses. For instance, research has shown that bodily sensations are not experienced naturally, as they really are, but are interpreted by the brain according to past experiences, parental conditioning and popular beliefs.

The now well developed science of biofeedback, which monitors the brain's response to stimuli, has shown that people can learn to influence voluntarily many kinds of bodily responses, such as slowing down the heartbeat, controlling blood pressure, and responding to pain.

Spiritual sex teaches you how to unlearn, transform, and recondition the body's responses during lovemaking.

Myth 4 — Sex is Only a Genital Affair. Most people's understanding of sex is limited to the genitals. Pioneer feminist Germaine Greer once observed, 'After all the porno flicks have been watched, all the sexual techniques applied, sex has not changed that much. It still boils down to ejaculating seminal fluid into a vagina.'

There is, however, another way. Spiritual sex teaches you that the ordinary orgasm of release is not the only goal of sexual intimacy. The whole body can be transformed into an erogenous zone, offering a multitude of erotic and sensual experiences that become increasingly subtle and ecstatic. Genital orgasm is the first step. Bliss is the last.

Myth 5 — Intercourse is the Only Meaningful Part of Sex. In present day culture all sexuality is directed toward the goal of intercourse.

Non-coital ways of enjoying sex have been downgraded as preparation only, or as immoral and unhealthy. The very word foreplay implies that sensual pleasures such as touching, stroking and kissing are relevant only within the context of sexual intercourse.

In spiritual sex you develop the art of prolonged non-coital eroticism to a highly refined degree, discovering that you can have full-body orgasms without penetration. This is a truth the ancient Tantric and Taoists master have long known and propounded.

Myth 6 — Your Sexual Pleasure Depends Upon Your Partner. The belief that you are dependent on a partner who is responsible for your sexual fulfilment is a widespread myth. It is based on the assumption that the source of your pleasure is not within you, but a result of what is done to you and how your lover does it.

Spiritual sex teaches you that you are responsible for your own sexual pleasure and that this realization is the first step in learning the art of ecstasy.

A person who has developed the ability to be orgasmic is naturally attractive to others, and more likely to find a mature partner for the further exploration of spiritual sex.

Myth 7 — In, Men, Orgasm Equals Ejaculation. As long as orgasm is thought to be the same as ejaculation (the Tantrics always knew them to be different), its biggest shortcoming will be the shortness of the act of coming usually from four to ten seconds.

Many people believe that the goal of lovemaking is to achieve the most intense possible release of sexual tension. This is particularly true for men, who are taught that sex without ejaculation is not worthwhile. Through understanding spiritual sex a man can gradually master his urge to ejaculate, so that he can decide when to release his semen instead of feeling it happen as an involuntary spasm. Men discover that they do not even have to ejaculate to feel sexually fulfiled. They can, in fact, like some women, experience multiple orgasms when they separate orgasm from ejaculation. This enables men to prolong lovemaking with their partners almost indefinitely.

It is possible for a man to have orgasms ranging from powerful genital vibrations to subtle streaming sensations through the whole body without emitting sperm. There is no sudden post ejaculation cut-off point that is normally experienced when men have released their seed.

Spiritual sex stresses the importance of prolonging pre-ejaculatory pleasure; a non-goal-oriented physical intimacy, enjoyed unhurriedly for its own sake, valuing exploration, intimacy, and sensitivity.

There's a lot more to Tantra than *sex.* It's about living in the now, being present in the moment, living neither in the past nor the future. Experiencing what is. Being consciously present.

My belief is that man first experienced the state of bliss during sex, the most natural no-mind state.

What is meditation? It can be defined as being intensely and totally present in the now. And this state was naturally experienced during the moments of our lovemaking and orgasms even by the most primitive man. It is almost as if nature had hard wired us to be meditative naturally and experience bliss, pleasure and pure consciousness.

When consciously attempted, anyone can learn how to stop the mind's incessant chatter and it's obsession with past and future, which constantly creates fear, pain and suffering.

So how do we become consciously present? We drop the mind. Just for a moment. Then we live our life moment by moment. To do this we will have to drop all conditioning that binds us. And this is where Tantra becomes so helpful and powerful. If we aspire to lasting happiness, which coincides with our full awakening in enlightenment, we must pay attention to our bodily existence here and now. We must become aware of our total reality in this present moment. Tantra takes the body seriously — not in the sense of granting it a finality that it does not have, but in understanding it as the ground for all realizations in the Now.

The Tantric approach to life is expressed well in the *Yoga-Vasihtha,* a remarkable Sanskrit work from thousands of years ago, which clearly states, 'For the ignorant person, this body is the source of endless suffering, but to the wise person, this body is the source of infinite delight. For the wise person, its loss is no loss at all, but while it persists it is completely a source of delight for the wise person. For the wise person, the body serves as a vehicle that can transport him swiftly in this world, and it is known as a chariot for attaining liberation and unending enjoyment. Since the body affords the wise person the experience of sound, sight, taste, touch and smell as well as prosperity and friendship, it brings him gain. Even though the body exposes one to a whole string of painful and joyous activities, the omniscient sage can patiently bear all experiences. The wise person reigns, free from feverish unhappiness, over the city known as the body.'

The body is the field in which we grow and harvest our experiences, which may be positive or negative, painful or pleasant. While negative, painful experiences do not bring us immediate joy, they do so in the long run because if we are wise we relate to them rightly by regarding them as useful lessons. No experience need be devoid of merit. People have had major spiritual breakthroughs as a result of deep suffering and debilitating illness. Even physical pain does not have to be a merely unpleasant experience. In fact, it can sometimes be a doorway to ecstasy.

To be clear, Tantra does not recommend that its initiates pursue pain. Its goal is that of all Indian liberation teachings: to move beyond all suffering and discover the indescribable bliss of Being. But Tantra understands that life on earth brings us mixed experiences to which we must apply a measure of dispassionate, patient acceptance and self-discipline. Fearful avoidance of what we think are negative experience merely strengthens this very attitude — namely, the exclusive identification with a limited body-mind — that breeds negative experiences. Likewise, blind attachment to what we consider positive experiences merely creates another kind of karmic bond by which we persist in our state of un-enlightenment.

Tantra asks us to go beyond the traditional stance of the cool, utterly detached observer of all our experiences. It recommends the more refined position of witnessing while at the same time understanding that observer and observed are not ultimately distinct. The Tantric approach is to see all life experiences as the play of the same One. Whether positive or negative, all experiences are embedded in absolute joy. When we have understood that what we dread the most — be it loss of health, property, relationships, or life itself — is not occurring to us but within our larger being, we begin to see the tremendous humour of embodiment. This insight is truly liberating.

The Tantric scriptures stress on what may be the most important discovery of ancient spirituality, namely, that we are the world. The world is our true body. The adepts of Tantra believe that it is possible to attain liberation, or enlightenment, even in the worst social and moral conditions. They also believe, however, that the traditional means devised or revealed in previous world ages are no longer useful or optimal, for those means were designed for people of far greater spiritual and moral stamina who lived in a more peaceful environment conducive to inner growth. The present age of 'high-tech and low-touch' darkness has innumerable obstacles that make spiritual maturation exceedingly difficult. Therefore, more drastic measures are needed.

One may question what is so special about the Tantric teachings that they should serve the spiritual needs of the Dark Age better than all other approaches? In many ways, the Tantric methods are similar to non-Tantric practices. What is strikingly different about them is their inclusiveness and the radical attitude with which they are pursued. A desperate person will grasp for a straw, and seekers in the *kali-yuga* (the present era, in Sanskrit called the age of darkness or ignorance) are, or should be, desperate. From the vantage point of a spiritual heritage extending over several thousand years, the Tantric masters at the beginning realized that the dark-age calls for especially powerful techniques to break through lethargy, resistance, and attachment to conventional relationships and worldly things, as well as to deal with the lack of understanding. Looking at the available means handed down from teacher to student through countless generations; they acknowledged that these required a purity and nobility of character that people of the Dark Age no longer possess.

To help humanity in the present era, the Tantric adepts modified the old teachings and created a whole new plethora of practices. Their orientation can be summed up in two words: Anything goes.

In Tantra, all the actions undertaken by the practitioner are means to the same end — the transformation of the individual and rebirth into a new level of consciousness.

Tantric Meditation 3

The Secret of Touch

It is difficult for us to touch our own bodies in a loving way. This is surprising, because really it is the most simple and natural thing to do: if you love yourself, then you love and respect your own body. But touching has been forbidden by most societies and small children quickly learn they should not touch themselves, unless there is something wrong with the body that needs attention.

Similarly, touching others is restricted. At the most, a mother can hug her child, a father can playfully wrestle with his son or daughter, but that is usually as far as touching goes in the early years, when these attitudes are formed.

If the body is not touched, it slowly becomes less and less sensitive. In Tantra, this sensitivity needs to be re-awakened, otherwise you will not be able to unlock the secrets of the body, especially in terms of experiencing your own energy and how it flows.

Touching each other's bodies is also a way of touching each other's energy. On an even deeper level it is can become a communion between two beings, two souls. Through touching your body, I can touch your heart and the physical connection is just a bridge. Then we are not two, we are merging into one, and this oneness can include everything — not just you and me, but this whole mysterious existence that surrounds us.

The First Stage. Sit facing your partner, about a metre (three feet) apart. Make sure you are comfortable and that your body is relaxed.

You can be naked or partly clothed. Some gentle background music and subdued lighting will help create the right ambience.

Softly gaze into each other's eyes. There is nothing to do. There is nothing special to be achieved or experienced. Do this for about ten minutes.

The Second Stage. Come close to your partner, so that your bodies are almost touching.

Close your eyes and let your hands and fingers touch your own body. Stroke yourself gently: on your hand, your arm, your face, on your whole body. Take your time. Explore in wonder your own landscape.

After about ten minutes, with eyes still closed, reach out with your hands to your partner and gently explore each other through touching. Let the touch be sensual rather than sexual. Imagine that your hands are the 'antennae' of your heart, so that really two hearts are touching each other.

After about ten minutes, stop and sit for a moment in silence, coming back to yourself. Keep your eyes closed. Without moving or touching yourself, feel your own body from inside, checking your own inner process and sensations. Perhaps you can feel that your own body is becoming more sensitive, more alive. Perhaps you can feel that energy is beginning to move.

When you feel ready, move your attention to your partner again and let your hands guide you in your exploration. When it feels right, melt in a loving embrace, completing the exercise.

Advanced Tantric Meditation 3

Humming for Lovers

This is a meditation method that can be enjoyed by a man and woman together.

It is a humming meditation, using sound as a way to move inwards. It can be a very beautiful way of preparing for an evening of Tantric lovemaking.

Light four small candles in the corners of your room or meditation space and burn your favourite incense.

Sit facing each other on cushions or a mattress, covering yourselves with a thin sheet, so it seems as if you are sitting together inside a 'tent'. It is best if you are naked under the tent.

Cross your hands and hold each other's hands. In this way, you are sitting holding hands, both with your arms crossed.

Close your eyes and hum, loudly enough so that you can hear each other.'

Continue for thirty minutes. Soon you will be able to feel that your two energies are melting and merging together.

When you have finished, remover the 'tent' and lie down quietly together in a soft embrace, not moving or doing anything, for at least fifteen minutes.

Then, after the silence, you can move into slow, sensual lovemaking.

4

Smell

'You've forgotten who you really are. And the day you ask 'who am I' is the day you begin the most wonderful journey there is — the journey back to the centre of creation.'

Advice from a Tantric Master

It is valuable to set aside special times to treat your lovemaking as a spiritual practice. Meditation, prayer, ritual and ceremony are common practices people use on a spiritual path. These can be combined in lovemaking by:

* Creating the right attitude. Say to your partner, 'Let's make love as a meditation today.' This creates the mind-set that everything you do in this particular session is for your spiritual growth.
* Creating a special space by placing ritual objects on a small table nearby — flowers, incense, candles, and other objects of spiritual significance for you.
* Sitting opposite each other and making a devotion. This is like a prayer in which you can say things such as 'may the good energy created by our lovemaking today be devoted to our bonding even closer together' or 'May this energy go the healing of my partner.'
* Having a common greeting that you say to each other each time you make love as a spiritual practice. Here is one that I use with my partner. You are welcome to use it if you wish or to make up

> one that means something special to you. 'I honour the Shakti within you and Shiva within me. I honour your love, your joy, and your pleasure. May our lovemaking today shine light on all things and may the angels of love be with us now.' We then ring a special ceremonial bell or light a candle to send our devotion out to the cosmos.

In the devotion Shakti represents the divine feminine energy within my partner and Shiva represents the masculine energy within me. In Hindu mythology it is written that through sexual union we can unite these two forces of the universe, Shakti and Shiva, and have tangible experience of the Divine.

One prevailing Hindu belief is that if you expressed the divinity within your loving union then you would manifest divinity in all aspects of your life. Another Hindu belief is that men and women are channels for God and Goddess. The way for a man to evoke this for himself is to treat his beloved as a goddess. So before I say — 'I honour the Shakti within you,' I look at my partner and I see beyond her personality, beyond her behaviour, beyond her looks and her actions. I see the goddess who resides in her. At that moment to me she is Shakti and I feel blessed to be in her presence. And as my partner honours the Shiva within me, I feel like Shiva at that moment.

When I say, 'I honour your love, your joy, and your pleasure,' I'm affirming to her that her love, her joy and her pleasure are spiritual qualities. When I say 'May our lovemaking shine light on all things,' I see the love we generate shining light on each other, our family and the world. The more we can love, the greater our gift to the cosmos.

When I say 'May the angels of love be with us now,' I think of the Tantric belief that when human beings have a deeply loving sexual experience, the angels of love from the cosmos are attracted to the intensity of their vibration.

Seeing the divinity within each other is not such an outrageous proposition. If you go into your lovemaking session with this mind-set it can create a whole new experience for you and broaden the spectrum of the way you make love. You can play with the idea of Shiva and Shakti and dress as a god and goddess for these special lovemaking sessions. It can be a lot of fun and spiritual growth should sometimes be fun.

Your sexuality is not only a vehicle to explore more love; it is also a vehicle for you to find a spiritual path.

Lovemaking can Become a Meditation

In meditation the mind is given something to focus on — sometimes the breath, sometimes a candle flame, sometimes a mantra (a sound you repeat over and over to yourself).

These are all techniques to still and focus the mind and direct the thoughts away from the swirls of daily life in order to experience a deep inner peace. Later in the book I give you several techniques that use the breath and certain muscles and that focus on the energy exchange between you and your partner to help keep the mind present in the moment during lovemaking. Meanwhile, here is a simple technique to start with.

Focusing on the Breath

Every time you find your mind drifting off or focusing on performance or becoming goal oriented, take your attention back to your breathing. Say, 'I am breathing in. I am breathing out,' or try coordinating your breathing with your partner's. Follow her breath so you are breathing as one body.

At first the techniques may seem to be creating the experience, but what is really creating it is your ability to be totally present. Your thoughts and feelings and your experience are all one.

Sexual ecstasy happens when you are so thoroughly absorbed in the richness of the present moment that nothing else exists.

What happens for most couples when they make love is that there are four 'people' present; you and your thoughts and your partner and her thoughts, and those thoughts very often are not on the moment at hand. When you are both focusing on the breath and the energy, both minds are attuned. It is possible to have an experience of being one body, one mind, one breath.

The techniques of breath focus and mind focus are very effective in creating a joint meditative experience. However, many people make the mistake of thinking it's the techniques that are creating these magical experiences, so they learn more and more mental techniques, adding *mantras* (sounds) and *yantras* (visual shapes and colours) and experimenting with all kinds of cycles of energy between each other. Their lovemaking becomes more and more a mind experience in which the whole natural beauty of sexual loving is lost. It is an essential attribute of Tantra to keep the practice simple and not allow the mind to get caught in complexities.

So, my advice is to always, and in all ways, keep it simple. In advanced stages of meditation you achieve a 'no mind' state — no program, no rehearsal, no goal, totally being in the present moment. The more familiar you are with the meditative lovemaking experience the easier it becomes to bring meditation naturally into your everyday lovemaking without constantly thinking about techniques.

If, while making love, you are aware that your mind is focusing on performance and result and not on the present moment, then you have the techniques to get you back into the present moment. Once your are in that moment again, forget the techniques, relax, let the breathing be slow and gentle and go with the flow of energy that is naturally happening. Don't force anything. Don't be goal oriented; be in the here and now as much as possible. Enjoy the meeting of the two bodies and two souls and melt into each other. If you find the mind drifting again or focusing on the result, gently bring it back with your breath. Be totally present again, feeling every sensation, every touch, every subtle movement of energy that happens.

In practising lovemaking as a meditation, you will go through four stages that normally occur when learning something new.

Stage 1: Unconscious incompetence — You are not aware that lovemaking can be a meditative experience and you have no skills to make it so.

Stage 2: Conscious incompetence — You become aware that you are not very good at being present with your lovemaking, that your mind is very often focusing on being able to satisfy your partner or on what you are going to do next or on comparing what's happening with a past experience and trying to repeat it.

Stage 3: Conscious competence — You are consciously bringing your mind into the present moment. You become very confident with the techniques of keeping your mind present on the energy exchange.

Stage 4: Unconscious competence — It happens naturally and you surrender totally to the flow of energy that is occurring between you. Your breathing is slow, you are relaxed and you've totally let-go. A deep silent communication happens between you; you melt into your beloved; your separate-ness disappears. You become one body; the lovemaking becomes less sexual and more spiritual and you remain in the experience of that awareness for hours. (It's usually found to be much easier for you to have this experience when your partner is on top because then you can relax more and surrender to receiving rather than doing.)

Making your Partner your Beloved

Tantra is about making love sacred, so, the partner is considered a beloved to be honoured, cherished and loved unconditionally.

Use the term 'beloved' when you speak to your partner and see how just the word alone arouses loving feelings. Say, 'John, my beloved, I would like to.....' When speaking about your partner to someone else, refer to him or her as 'My beloved'. It might seem strange at first, but you will also be sending out that loving energy to the person with whom you are speaking, who will share in that love.

You will see an amazing shift in attitude, both in yourself and in your partner, if you continue this simple practice.

Tantra is a path to Divinity, both within and without — the feeling of divine blessing and presence in every aspect of your life, including sex. This connection with the divine is achieved by ecstatic union with a beloved as you both experience your own — and each other's divinity.

In Tantra, every man and woman is a god or goddess. That means you are a divine being just as you are, with wisdom and abilities that need only to be recognized and released. Honouring yourself and being honoured in this way gives us the self-esteem we all need but often feel lacking. Once you see the divinity within yourself, you can see the divinity in others.

Through my years of work as a spiritual guide, I know how happy people become when they are acknowledged. Do you know what it feels like to be truly appreciated? To be really noticed? To be deeply known?

Tantric sex takes acknowledgement one step further: to being worshipped! Worship doesn't mean blind obsession, it means loving unconditionally and limitlessly. Nor does it mean having power over someone who is your slave, it means serving each other equally from the highest state of personal power and mutual respect.

Nine Blessings of Tantric Sexual Practices

There are many dividends from investing time and energy into Tantric sex. Tantric sex awareness and practices can help you achieve at least the following:-

1. Expand Your Possibilities for Love. Tantric sex shows you how to deepen the physical and spiritual connection with your partner, and nurture and love yourself.

2. Rejuvenate Your Health. Practising Tantric sex has physiological and psychological effects that maintain and regain health. For example, breathing techniques bring more air into the body, nourishing the tissue and muscles. Research has shown a link between the effects of relaxation, meditation, and spirituality and better physical and emotional health. People who are spiritual have lower blood pressure, lower levels of anxiety and depression, more stable hormone levels, and better functioning immune systems.

3. Remain Youthful. For all health benefits mentioned previously, practising Tantra can make you feel and look young again.

4. Empower Women and Men. Many women suffer from low self-esteem. They might have a poor body image or they might give into sex when they would really like to say no or not tell their partner what they really want. In Tantric sex, women are treated with the respect and honour they desire and deserve. So many men worry about their penis size, and how long they last in sex. Many also don't know how to commit to or really please a woman. When men feel more empowered in sex, they become more confident and open to being more caring in their relationship.

5. Help You Achieve True Satisfaction From Sex. When the sex act is over, are you ever left with the feeling that you're not really finished? This is often because the sexual act does not go beyond the genitals — it does not touch the heart. In Tantra you will feel fulfiled from the soul connection you develop with your partner. When sex happens with this kind of heart connection, both body and mind are fed.

6. Alleviate Anxieties and Depression. Statistics show millions of men and women suffer from anxiety and depression, including symptoms like fatigue, listlessness and sleeping and eating disturbances. Tantric sex provides an enormous source of energy to the body and peacefulness to the mind that overcomes these problems.

7. Elevate Sex. When you elevate sex to a level of sacredness, it takes on a richer dimension than a mere physical act.

8. Prolong Pleasure. Tantric sex techniques make lovemaking — including the afterglow — last a long time. This occurs not only through ejaculatory control but by learning to direct sexual energy anywhere in the body or into spiritual manifestations.

9. Heal Past Emotional Wounds. Tantric sex can help you heal past hurts from all kinds of painful or traumatic experiences in which you felt betrayed or abused. Instead, it helps you create experiences of being honoured and respected in sex and in life in general.

If you want to understand the movement of energy within you better and also how to use it as a vehicle towards your own self-realization, it is imperative that you have a working knowledge about the chakra system of the human body.

Chakras — Wheels of Life

Physicists agree that everything in our world is energy. Think of how we talk about being drawn to someone 'like a magnet' or feel electricity in their presence — all signs of energy.

According to Tantric philosophy, energy centres known as chakras go along an imaginary axis down the core of our physical body from the bottom of our pelvis to top of our head. These are not physical entities but subtle energy fields associated with different quantities. If you could see them, they would look like energy forces spinning in a wheel out of seven different centres in your body. Being familiar with these chakras is crucial to understanding the presence and movement of life-energy within your body.

The following chakra chart shows the colours, sounds, and issues associated with each energy centre. The questions in the chart reveal whether you have strength or blocks in that area. The idea is to focus on a particular chakra (area of your body) and recite the sound associated with it, or think about the particular colour, to connect with the energy in that centre.

Another approach in using this chart is to read the issues and questions and see which ones are relevant to you (either that you feel good or bad about them). Then focus on the chakra, colour and sound in order to strengthen yourself regarding that issue. For example, if you're feeling stifled in expressing yourself (the fifth chakra), put your hand on your throat, visualize the colour blue, and repeat the sound '*ham*' to give yourself more courage to speak up.

All breathing practices, done consciously, help you create a clear channel in your body through which air and energy can travel past these chakras, cleansing, feeding, and fuelling you. Air going through a clear channel in your body is called an inner flute because of its sweet flute-like sound.

You then can send your breath to your partner, who will cycle it through his or her chakras and return it, fuelling and empowering you both.

As you breathe, picture the breath going through the chakras. Try the following exercises.

The complete breath. This works to totally relax you. Inhale deeply into your lower belly and chest (until it pouches out like a contended Buddha). You can do this on your own or with a partner, either face to face or back to back. Sadly, many people resist doing this breath, feeling unattractive with their belly popping out, but it is a good breath to do in the middle of sex. Say, 'Let's do the Buddha breath', and press your bellies and chests against each other.

The fire breath. In contrast, as its name suggests, the fire breath fires you up. Take continual rapid breaths in and out of the nose (like snorting) causing your stomach to pulsate quickly. You can accelerate the energy more by raising and lowering your arms.

Once you get your individual breathing going better, you are ready to breathe with a partner for more powerful love connections. One word of caution, however: Too much energy in the brain before you are prepared to handle it can cause you to literally 'blow your fuse' like too many electrical appliances in an outlet. This results in headaches, confusion, passing out, or even a panic attack.

Synchronizing breath. In this exercise you breathe in and out at the same times as your partner to get on the same wavelength. Sit comfortably cross-legged facing each other. Use a wink or touch to signal your pacing. After a while, close your eyes to sense each other's energy pattern.

Reciprocal breath. In this breath imagine that you are exchanging air, inhaling your partner's breath (or imagine breathing for each other). Sit in the yab-yum position (woman sitting on man's lap, facing each other, genitals in contact and mouths opposite each other) and inhale while your partner exhales, then exhale while your partner inhales.

Circulating breath. For this breath, inhale, imagining energy rising up from your sex centre (second chakra) through your body (passing through all the chakras, as listed in the previous table), travelling to the top of your head, then back down to your genitals and the base of your spine on the exhale. Picture tracing a loop inside yourself and then out to a partner. Practices can be called by different names by different

Chakra Chart Evaluation

Chakra	Colour	Mantra	Issue	Question(s)
1. Base	Red	Lam	Security	Do you feel insecure, needy, and helpless? Or safe, secure, grounded?
2. Sex	Orange	Vam	Energy	Do you feel undesirable and inhibited? Or sexy and alive?
3. Solar Plexus	Yellow	Ram	Power	Do you feel threatened weak, and powerless? Or confident and worthy?
4. Heart	Green	Yam	Expression	Do you feel unloved and abandoned? Or loving and compassionate?
5. Throat	Blue	Ham	Expression	Do you feel unheard, misunderstood, and passive? Or expressive and truthful?
6. Third Eye	Purple	Ooo	Vision	Do you feel unclear, unauthentic confused? Or inspired and intuitive?
7. Crown	Violet	Omm	Enlightenment	Do you feel spiritually void and disconnected? Or enlightened, ecstatic, and cosmically connected?

disciplines. For example, the Tantric Circulating Breath is known to Chinese Taoists as the Microcosmic Orbit or the Golden Circle.

Bliss breath. Inhale deeply through your mouth and exhale naturally and continuously, allowing any natural sounds. Smile.

Ecstatic breathing. To do this breath, lie on your back with your knees up and inhale long, slow breaths through the mouth, counting to five, expanding the abdomen, and creating an archway under the small of the back. Exhale to the count of five, bringing your back to the floor and

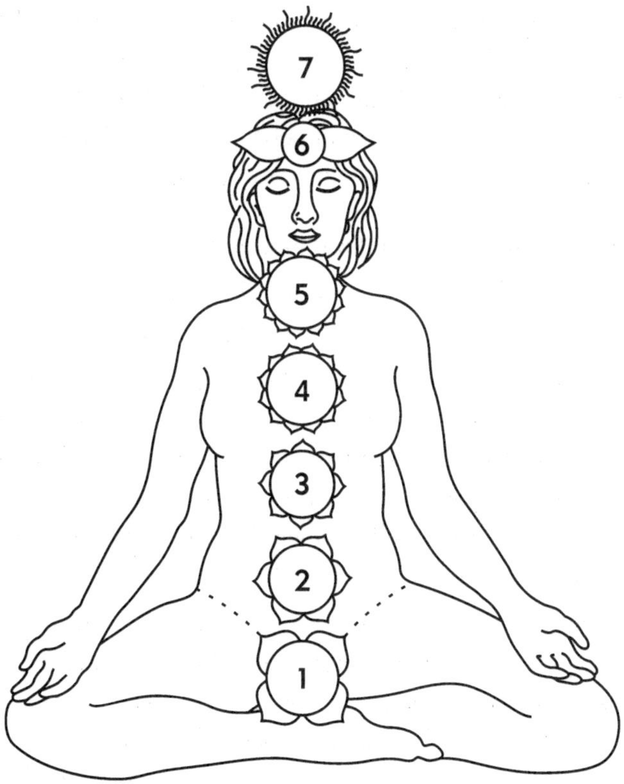

The Seven Chakras

tilting your pelvis slightly upward. Allow the air to rush into the chest, opening your throat. Repeat rhythmically to create a wave-like motion throughout the body. Release any tightness in the throat, neck, chest, shoulders, abdomen, buttocks, or pelvis by purposefully tightening and then releasing the muscles in those areas. Allow sounds and feelings (sadness, anger, joy) to emerge freely on the exhale.

Partner pelvic passion breath. This breath is named this because it really perks up your passion by intensifying the energy created by the circulating breath with the pelvic holds. An additional benefit results from pressing your heart chakras together. Lie side by side or sit face to face with the woman in the man's lap (yab yum position). Keep eye contact while you inhale and exhale together to a count of five, and draw the breath up from the base of your spine to the top of the head, and back down again. Create a cycle of breath with one of you inhaling while the other exhales. Imagine sending love out to your partner's breath. Gently press your heart areas together. You can heighten or lessen your arousal by pumping your pelvic muscles to force more breath — and therefore more energy — into your body.

First Chakra: Rooting/ Grounding/ Foundation

When the first chakra is open, you will feel secure, calm, and motivated. You will welcome change, and adapt well to new circumstances.

The adrenal glands regulate the flight or fight reaction in response to threats and danger with release of two hormones, epinephrine (adrenaline) and norepinephrine (noradrenaline). The adrenals determine how well you manage stress of any kind in your life. When your body manages stress well, you will have courage and calmness in the face of threats or danger and be able to act fearlessly.

When the first chakra is blocked or closed, you will feel insecure and may experience paranoia. Change will be threatening to you. Life seems beyond your control so you may try to compensate by over controlling little things, for example always eating at exactly the same time each day, always sitting in the same chair — 'your chair'. You may become fanatical about orderliness or cleanliness. You will tend to be incapacitated in the face of danger. You may bully those who are weaker and more vulnerable than you are.

Opening the First Chakra

You can stimulate any chakra, help it to open and encourage it to spin, rotate, or vibrate by touching it. You can touch yourself or your partner can touch you, and vice versa.

* Lie on your right side. This will tend to open your left nostril and stimulate your right brain hemisphere.
* Reach around from behind and place your left palm on your sacrum (tailbone) with your middle finger (the longest finger) touching your coccyx.
* Reach around from the front and place your right palm on your perineum and your middle finger touching the middle finger of your left hand at your coccyx. In this position you are reaching down between your crotch, one hand from the front and one hand from the rear until your two longest fingers just touch, and with the rest of your hands against your skin.
* You can do this while clothed or naked; being naked is more powerful.
* Hold this position while you visualize the colour red, and make the sound '*lam*' (long vowel '*aaaaa*').
* You may also place any red, black, brown, or silver stone or crystal between your hands and your body while you do this meditation.
* Visualize the energy in this chakra spinning, for example, smoke or fog swirling in a clockwise direction, or a propeller rotating in a clockwise direction.

Second Chakra: Navel/Belly/Sexuality Chakra

The second chakra is located at the belly, or hara, in the centre of the space between your hipbones, about two finger widths below the navel.

This chakra is the *Svadhisthana* Chakra (The place of the senses). The sound of this chakra is VAM, the colour of this chakra is orange. The body organs most closely associated with this chakra are the kidneys, bladder, small intestine, and large intestine (including the colon, rectum, and anal canal). Specifically for men, this includes: prostate, penis, scrotum, and testicles; for women: vagina, uterus, and ovaries.

When the second chakra is open and vibrating, you will feel confident and balanced, trusting that the universe will provide all that you need because you actually experience abundance. You will attract money and success easily and so will act with generosity toward others. You will feel comfortable with your sexuality, experiencing great passion. Men will be able to get and maintain erections. Women will be easily orgasmic.

When the second chakra is blocked or closed, you may be stingy and protective of what you have out of fear that you will lose it and not be able to get more. You may be overly materialistic, and not having enough money will be a constant worry. You may experience a lot of fear and this may be associated with health problems in the body organs associated with this chakra, for example, kidney infections, or a lot of grief getting an erection, or may suffer from premature ejaculation. Women may have difficulty allowing themselves to surrender enough to become orgasmic.

Opening the Second Chakra

* Open your hands, keeping your fingers together and extend your thumb at a right angle to your fingers. If you look at your right hand when it is open this way, your index finger and your thumb form an 'L' shape, and your left hand forms a reverse 'L' shape.
* Place your thumbs on your hips, right thumb on right hip and left thumb on left hip. Bring your open hands around your front covering your abdomen until the longest finger on each hand just touches each other.

* Alternatively, bring your hands around your back until your longest finger on each hand just touches each other.
* Holding your hands in either of these positions brings healing energy to these organs and stimulates the second chakra. You can also lightly massage the area for additional stimulation. This is excellent for rejuvenating the kidneys and relieving lower back pain.
* Hold this position while you visualize the colour orange, and make the sound '*vam*' (long vowel '*aaaaa*').
* You may place any orange objects, for example crystals, flowers, or cloth, between your hands and your body while you do this meditation. Visualize the energy in this chakra spinning, swirling in a clockwise direction, or a propeller rotating in a clockwise direction.

Third Chakra: Will/Solar Plexus Chakra

The third chakra is at the solar plexus located in the space from about one inch above your belly button up to the indentation of your breastplate, but not as high as between your breasts.

This is the Manipura Chakra (The city of the Jewel). The sound of this chakra is '*ram*'. The colour of this chakra is yellow. The body parts most closely associated with this chakra are the stomach, pancreas, spleen, liver, and gall bladder, the muscular system, and the skin as a system.

The third chakra is the centre of your will.

When the third chakra is open, you will be at ease in your body. Emotionally balanced, you will feel everything fully, both positive and negative emotions, but you will not be consumed by them. Self-motivated, you will be able to express your will in a way that is free of ego, getting what you want without placing anyone else at a disadvantage. You will be a good decision-maker and problem-solver, radiating a charisma that leads others to select you as a leader. You will be tolerant of those who have different viewpoints, lifestyles, values, and appearances from your own.

When the third chakra is closed, you will be unhappy with your body, perceiving it as too short, tall, skinny, fat, ugly, and so on, even though this may have nothing to do with any objective reality. Wildly enthusiastic one minute and depressed the next, you may experience life as an emotional roller coaster. Emotions may overwhelm you, or you may have closed them off and feel nothing at all. Struggle for power and influence may consume you. Certain that no one listens to you, you may feel that you have to prove yourself all the time. Worrying a lot, you may make selfish decisions without considering how those decisions affect others. Lack of motivation, depression, frustration, and tiredness may be your norm. Judgemental of others who have different viewpoints, lifestyles, values, and appearances from your own, you may openly ridicule them. You may experience liver problems and constipation because of repressed anger, or problems with your spleen, stomach, or pancreas due to excessive worry.

Opening the Third Chakra

* Gently thump your solar plexus with your open palm. Do not thump so hard that you bruise yourself or that it is uncomfortable. Thump in this manner 10 to 15 times.
* Then rub your hand, palm open, in a clockwise direction over the solar plexus for one minute. You can also do this for your lover.
* While you are rubbing your hand on the solar plexus chakra, visualize the colour yellow, and make the sound ram (long vowel aaaaa).
* You may place any yellow objects, for example crystals, flowers, or cloth; between your hands and your body while you do this meditation.
* Visualize the energy in this chakra spinning, for example, smoke or fog swirling in a clockwise direction, or a propeller rotating in a clockwise direction.

Fourth Chakra: Heart/Love Chakra

The fourth chakra is located at the spot between your nipples at arm-pit level.

This is the Anahata Chakra. The sound of this chakra is '*yam*'. The colour of this chakra is green.

The body parts most closely associated with this chakra are the heart, breasts, lungs, thymus gland, and the cardiovascular blood circulation system.

When the fourth chakra is open, you will freely give and receive both romantic and unconditional love, easily forgiving hurts and extending compassion to all. Trustworthy and reliable, you will have a deep capacity for commitment. In the now moment, richly aware of your senses, you will also be in touch with your feelings, both positive and negative.

Relationships will be high priorities for you and you will have strong connections to family and community. You will be happy in spite of the circumstances of your life rather than because of them, laughing frequently and sharing your joy. You will experience sublime moments of sexual ecstasy with your lover. For you, the glass is half full rather than half empty. Because the thymus gland is critical to immune system function, you will tend to be healthy most of the time, rarely getting sick, or healing quickly when you do.

When the fourth chakra is blocked or closed, you will have great difficulty in relationships, both friendships and romances. To protect yourself from being hurt or wounded as you were in previous relationships, you will remain emotionally closed. As you shut down your feelings, life may become dull and predictable. You may experience profound alienation from your lover, your children, your friends, your neighbours, and your peers at work, because you feel they do not understand you and disapprove of you. You may be alone, or move from one relationship to another as they disappoint you and fail. Rather than seeing that the root of your sadness is inside yourself, you blame your unhappiness on circumstances and other people.

Thinking, reason, and intellect are your refuge. You can lose yourself completely in your work. For you, the glass is half empty rather than half full. Your grief may bring on lung disorders. To the extent that the blockage in this chakra affects your thymus gland, your immune system will not function optimally and you may find that you get sick easily and often and heal slowly.

Opening the Fourth Chakra

* With a set of coloured pencils, draw a picture that illustrates how your heart is closed, protected, and shielded from negative feelings and emotions. For example you might draw your heart encased in a block of ice, or barricaded behind a wall of bricks and mortar, or enclosed in a suit of armour, or whatever image comes to mind for you.
* Lie down on your back with your chest bare.
* Dilute one drop of rose essential oil in one teaspoon of vegetable oil. Touch the fingertips of your left hand into the mixture and anoint your heart chakra by massaging the oil gently into your skin, circling your fingers in a clockwise direction.
* Put a piece of green silk on your heart chakra. Place several green stones (for example, jade or emerald) on top of the silk. If you have any rose petals, preferably fresh, place those on the green silk also.
* Place your left palm covering the objects on your heart chakra, and place the right palm covering the left palm.
* Softly chant the sound '*yam*' (long vowel '*aaaaa*') as a mantra for four minutes.
* Repeat this exercise four days in a row. Gently wash the silk by hand after each repetition of the exercise to remove any residual oil it may have absorbed.
* The drawing of your heart is only done on day one and again on day four. There will likely be a noticeable difference in how you draw your heart on the fourth day, for example, the wall may be

crumbling or the armour may have holes appear in it, or the ice may be melting or completely gone as you begin to open your heart to experience all emotions.

Fifth Chakra: Throat/Neck/Communication Chakra

The fifth chakra is located at the centre of the throat at the level of a man's Adam's apple. This is the Vishudda Chakra. The sound of this chakra is '*ham*'. The colour of this chakra is sky-blue. The body parts most closely associated with the fifth chakra are the throat, thyroid gland, and parathyroid glands.

When the fifth chakra is open, you will find your voice, expressing yourself easily and clearly both verbally and nonverbally. You may take pleasure in singing and whistling. Sound may seem to have magical qualities to it and certain sounds will easily transport you into a delightfully altered, expanded consciousness. You will be a lover of music, perhaps making your own, either writing music or playing instruments.

With no difficulty in expressing your point of view, you will easily take a stand on issues of importance to you and be known as a person who speaks the truth. A quick thinker and articulate speaker, you will be excited by ideas and take pleasure in the matching of wits with others in debate.

The thyroid gland acts as the body's 'accelerator pedal'. It speeds up the metabolic rate and the rate of chemical reactions inside cells, and this powerfully influences your energy level. When this chakra is open and the thyroid is healthy, you will easily maintain your ideal body weight without the need to carefully monitor what you eat, and you will generally feel full of energy and motivation.

If the fifth chakra is blocked or closed, you will find difficulty expressing your ideas and opinions. Speaking in front of people will make you nervous and writing will be difficult and frustrating. You will avoid taking a firm stand or position on controversial subjects, usually waiting for someone else to lead the way. Once someone else has articulated a firm position, you will tend to agree with that person and adopt the point of view as your own. You may change your mind a lot about many things, so that it is hard for others to know what you believe in.

Because you are much more comfortable when everyone agrees with each other, disagreements, discussions, and even friendly arguments may frighten you. You may speak either very softly or very loudly, or you may mumble a lot. You may be apologetic for what you say or you may end many of your sentences with a rise in inflection, thus turning each one into a question, even when you are stating a fact, You may have a distinct preference for feeling and be distrustful of what you consider to be an overemphasis upon thinking.

When this chakra is blocked, you may find that it is very difficult to control your weight even though you pay careful attention to what and how much you eat. The parathyroid glands control calcium in the blood. If you are having problems with osteoporosis which is a loss of bone density with ageing (most common with the onset of menopause in women), you may wish to concentrate on opening this chakra.

Opening the Fifth Chakra

* Alone or with a partner, make chanting sounds.
* Work your voice up and down the octave scale.
* The sound ham (long vowel aaaaa) is a good one to use.
* You may experiment with closing your eyes and visualizing blue as you chant.
* If you are with a partner, bring your chanting into harmony with each other.
* Do this daily.

Sixth Chakra: Forehead/Third Eye/Intuition Chakra

The sixth chakra is located at the forehead and is often referred to as the third eye. This is the *Ajna* Chakra. The sound of this chakra is AUM. The colour of this chakra is indigo (deep blue). The body parts most closely associated with this chakra are the pituitary gland (the master gland) and the pineal gland.

When the sixth chakra is open and vibrating, you will have an ability to 'see' or understand what is actually going on in any set of circumstances very quickly. Blessed with insight, you will know what to do or not to do in almost any situation.

You will exhibit wisdom, a quality beyond intellect, knowledge, or experience. You will have vision, the ability to imagine how the future could be, and thereby gain considerable influence over how the future actually turns out. You will consistently be able to create the results that you vividly imagine.

In spite of this, you may not be particularly goal-oriented, in the usual way that people set goals and then rely upon their willpower to achieve success. Rather, you will operate with faith in your higher self and in God that the universe is a place of abundance, and if you are doing your life's work, you will be supported along the way. Your life tends to be filled with amazement, astonishment, surprise, and delight, as what the universe presents to you is beyond anything your ego could have worked to create with willpower.

You may have regular mystical/religious experiences, for example, *satori* or *samadhi,* that go beyond rational description, and you may be blessed with various forms of ESP (extra sensory perception) or other special powers.

You are the beneficiary of what we call the positive time paradox. Living in the now moment, you move slowly, yet time seems to fly by because you so thoroughly enjoy almost everything you do. In spite of this, you seem have plenty of time to get everything done.

The pituitary gland regulates a number of key hormones including growth hormone, estrogen, progesterone, prolactin, oxytocin, and testosterone. If this chakra is open, you may find that you age gracefully and perhaps more slowly than others your same age, and that you maintain a high level of libido and sexual stamina. The pineal gland primarily regulates the sleep cycle. If this chakra is open, you will be able to sleep well and awaken fully rested.

When the sixth chakra is blocked or closed, you will place great importance upon education, acquired knowledge, and experience.

You will rely upon your willpower to get what you want. You will feel reluctant to rely upon others, preferring to do everything for yourself. You may have a strong sense that only you can do it well enough or right.

You may have trouble even saying the word 'God', let alone to rely in faith that what you need will come to you in some mysterious way. You may be strongly goal-oriented, creating a clear image in your mind of what you want to achieve, and then systematically plotting a course to achieve the success you want. You may indeed be highly successful at getting results, which confirms that what you are doing works. Your life has few surprises and little mystery. You are extremely skeptical of those claiming to have mystical experiences, and probably strongly deny the existence of any form of ESP.

You are the victim of what we call the negative time paradox. Most of the time, you are busy doing, and the very idea of just being seems like a boring waste of time. You may have a tendency to be a hyperactive workaholic. You move rapidly, but time seems to go too slowly, in the sense that you are always eager for some future result you are pursuing, and easily become impatient with the steps needed to get you there. Paradoxically, at the same time your never seem to have enough time to get everything done.

You may find that you age prematurely compared with others your same age. People might say that age was not kind to you. You may experience little interest in sexuality, instead channelling your energies elsewhere, for example into your work, as a diversion. You may regularly have trouble sleeping or find that your sleep is easily interfered with, and that jet lag is severe when you travel.

Opening the Sixth Chakra

* Lightly massage the third eye spot, the centre of your forehead, with the first two fingers of either hand.
* Rotate your fingers first in a counter-clockwise direction and then in a clockwise direction nine times.

* Visualize the colour purple and make the sound '*aum*' (long vowel '*auuuuu*').
* Do three, six, or nine repetitions of this exercise daily.

Seventh Chakra: Enlightenment/Crown Chakra

The seventh chakra is the crown chakra located at the top of your head. It is called the *Sahasrar* chakra (the thousand petalled lotus). The sound of this chakra is '*ah*'. The colour of this chakra is white or violet. The body parts most closely associated with the crown chakra are the central nervous system (brain and spinal cord) and the peripheral nervous system. The peripheral nervous system consists of sensory neurons that carry sensory input from receptors to the CNS (central nervous system), and motor neurons that transmit motor output from the CNS to muscles and glands.

When the seventh chakra is truly fully open and vibrating, you will be whole again.

You will know what it means to live in a state of grace. The Kundalini serpent — a metaphor for pure consiciousness and life force energy within you — will be uncoiled and released flowing freely up from the earth, through all seven of your chakras, out from your crown, up to the heavens, and back down again at a high mystical rate of vibration.

Your meditations will sometimes transport you into contemplative states in which the boundary between yourself and others will disappear. You will come face to face with the Creator, God, or the Divine in high states of *satori*, *samadhi*, and enlightenment. You may experience and possibly even perform miracles such as healing yourself and others. Your faith will be inviolable. You will operate in the world from a context of unconditional love and compassion for all sentient beings. You will be beyond desire, wanting, and karma. You will be free.

When the seventh chakra is blocked or closed, you will be very much caught in the endless cycle of birth and death, subject to the laws of karma. You may long to return home to God, but direct mystical experiences mostly elude you.

You are still trying to make them happen and have not learned to surrender to allow them to happen. Intellectually, you may understand that the lower cannot command the higher, but you repeatedly fall back upon what you know how to do. Your ego regularly gets the front seat in your consciousness and your higher self recedes into the background. You have to work hard at reconfirming your faith, and it sometimes fails you completely.

Regardless of your level of achievement and success in the world (power, position, wealth, sex), you are still prone to periods of spiritual darkness and fear of death. This compels you to try and get more of what you already have, even though you already have enough. You are still quite capable of operating selfishly and perhaps even violently toward your fellow man, even (or perhaps especially) those closest to you, including friends and family.

You may be the envy of your peers because of your worldly success, but inside you still often feel like a fraud or a fake. You ask yourself repeatedly, 'Is this all there is?'

Once you become aware of your male and female energy, how do you balance them? All the Tantric practices mentioned in this book help you to do that. Be patient; this achievement takes times. Meanwhile, there are several simple ways to balance those energies. Here are six of the simplest but effective ways to balance sexual energy:

Nostril Breathing. You can control the balance of your male or female energy by choosing which nostril to block or open. To stimulate more male (yang) energy (active, analytical, assertive), block your left nostril and breathe only through your right nostril. To stimulate more feminine (yin) energy (receptive, passive, nurturing), block your right nostril and breathe through your left nostril. You can also turn your head to the left to be more in your male energy; this assists in breathing through your right nostril. Turn to the right to activate more female energy.

Alternate Nostril Breathing. This is a common exercise in yoga classes. Sit quietly. Put your right index finger on your third eye and rest your thumb and middle finger on your nostrils. Exhale forcefully and then close one nostril with your finger and inhale through the other nostril to the count of seven. Then close that nostril while releasing the other nostril and breathe through the open nostril to the count of seven. Without pausing, continue alternately closing and opening the nostrils as you breathe. In more advanced practice, you would also contract the PC muscles to create more force in the breath.

Use Different Sounds. Chant '*om*' to stimulate more male energy and '*aum*' for more female energy. Then chant the two sounds alternately for several minutes until you feel the sounds are merging.

Focus on Symbols of Male or Female. The Star of David, commonly identified as a symbol of the Jewish religion, is actually an ancient Tantric meditation design, with the two intersecting triangles symbolizing the male and female, mind and body. The points on the Star of David also symbolize the sex organs, with the penis and vagina at the upper and lower tips, the breasts at either end of the top line, and the testicles at either end of the lower line.

Focus on Colours. Male energy is cool, logical blue, and female energy is emotional, passionate red, so surround yourself with either colour. Mentally focus on red or blue, look at an item coloured red or blue, or purposefully put on red or blue clothing.

Move your Body. To draw in more male energy, sweep your hands out from your sides over your head, into the sky; looking up, imagine calling in the energy from the sky. For more female energy, bend down slightly and scoop the energy up from mother earth and into your heart. In a variation of this, use just the right arm to sweep the sky and the left hand to sweep the earth while keeping the other hand on whatever energy centre you want to empower.

Tantra asks you to arrive at your own sense of balance, both inner and outer, through experimenting and actual experience. However, it also has created powerful ways to assist you in this arrival at harmony and thus to hasten your journey to the final goal of Bliss and Freedom. Here is one of Tantra's gems, called the Polarity Practice:

The Tantric Polarity Technique

The Tantric Polarity Process is designed to bring the body into a balanced state before sex. The benefits are better health, total relaxation, and better and longer orgasms, and it also builds trust and intimacy between partners.

As I explained earlier, there are many energy centres or bioelectric vortexes in the body called the chakras, or Wheels of Light — seven primary psycho-energetic vortices each having a particular function in the body, but the most important is the heart chakra, *Anahata.*

There are three charkas above the heart chakra and three below. Thus the heart chakra is the very centre of the human being, and also meant to be the foundation of his existence.

The tree chakras above have to do with intellect and spirituality.

The three chakras below deal with the basic human needs and emotions.

The *Anahata* balances the spirit with the body — this chakra is the seat of unconditional love and divine grace.

The technique takes about 50 minutes and each step no more than five minutes.

Start with deep breathing to feel relaxed, unrushed, aware and focused on loving the other. One becomes the 'receiver', and the other, the 'giver'.

The receiver lies naked, flat on his back, legs spread comfortably apart.

The giver sits cross-legged, on the right side of the receiver, kneeling slightly touching the receiver's body.

The giver positions herself so that she can reach her partner's genitals with the right hand and the top of her partner's head with the left. The key is for the giver to find a comfortable position so she doesn't need to move her body during the process.

Both giver and receiver spend about five minutes focusing on deep, relaxing, breathing, and letting go of anxiety.

The giver rubs her hands together, warming them, then shakes them away from the receiver's body, flicking the fingers and visualizing energy sparking from them. It energizes the hands, preparing them for contact with the receiver's body.

The giver then places her left hand, negatively charged, gently on the receiver's Heart chakra, in the centre of the chest, between the nipples — in Tantra this is the most intimate and beautiful part of the body, the centre and seat of divine essence.

The giver then places her right hand — positively charged — gently on the receiver's root chakra, between the anus and genitals — the perineum, which is the foundation of survival and human needs such as food, shelter, money, and the place from where the *kundalini* rises.

The giver keeps her hands in place for five minutes, visualizing energy coming from the earth and the universe, flowing through her body and streaming out of her hands into her partner's body, and conscious of the healing power inherent in all human beings and in all animate and inanimate forms.

Now, keeping her left hand on the receiver's heart, she moves her right hand to his genitals, cupping them — the seat of sexual desire and procreative power — for five minutes, occasionally applying gentle pressure or slight movement to awaken this chakra.

Sexual arousal often indicates energy is being received.

Now, she moves her right hand to just below the receiver's navel — the centre of his personal power — keeping the left hand on his heart chakra, for five minutes.

This is balancing the three lower chakras with the heart chakras, bringing divine love and wisdom into the system.

Moving her right hand on top of her left hand she keeps both hands on the receiver's heart for five minutes, focusing on all she has to give as a friend, a healer and a lover, and visualizing it flowing from her hands into his heart.

Next, the giver moves her left hand to the receiver's throat — the seat of his creative and communicative power — resting it gently, while the right hand remains on the heart, for five minutes.

Then she places her left hand on the receiver's forehead — the seat of his intellect and psychic power — for five minutes.

Then she moves her left hand to the top or crown of the receiver's head — his connection to the divine and spiritual levels — for five minutes, then slowly takes both hands off the receiver's body and moves away from him — while he remains totally relaxed, eyes closed — and shakes her hands and flicks her fingers.

After five minutes the giver and the receiver change places, and the receiver becomes the giver.

When both have completed the process, lovemaking begins.

The Value of Taking Turns at Pleasure

This is another great Tantric secret. And even though taking turns at pleasing and being pleased might sound programmed, this technique has also proven successful in many sex therapies. I've believed in it for years, as it is highly effective; particularly because so many women worry, 'When is my turn up?' and 'Have I taken too much time?' and because many men fret, 'Have I performed well?' and 'Have I really pleased her?'

Taking turns is crucial in some Tantric lovemaking practices to allow full focus on either giving or receiving without worrying about taking too much time, being selfish, or your partner getting tired. Ultimately, when the energy of lovemaking is truly flowing, the partners are so intertwined that it's hard to distinguish who is giving and who is receiving. **Body parts and souls merge into one and into universal consciousness.** The receiver and giver blend into one. Choose one night when she will be the total receiver and you will the full-on giver, attending to her every need and delight. Choose another night when it is your turn to receive all of her undivided attention.

All the senses are honoured in Tantric lovemaking. That means all the organs involved with these senses are also centres of the body. Here are some examples of exercises you can do with your partner to create bliss between you that activates each of the senses:

Mouth and Face. Trace around your beloved's mouth with your fingertips and pull the lips apart gently. The lips are related to the genitals, according to Eastern tradition, and licking and sucking them can stimulate the sexual organs. Press your lips to your partner's and make motions. Extend your touch to the area around the mouth and to the cheeks and face. Blindfold your partner and feed him or her various tasty morsels with different textures (try strawberries, chocolate-covered cherries or a spoonful of ice cream). Tantalize your partner as you do this.

Eyes. The eyes truly are the window to the soul, and earlier I mentioned the importance of eye gazing as fundamental to all Tantric connecting. Go a step further by touching your partner's eyes gently around the eye sockets and across the lids, making circles at the corners and tracing out to the temples. Let your gaze roam from each other's eyes down to other parts with wonder and appreciation.

Nose. The nose is cherished in Tantric practice, since along with the mouth it the entrance for the vital breath that is the life force (called *prana*). Besides, its function (scent) plays a vital role in attraction! Stimulate your partner's sense of smell by blindfolding him or her and passing various scents (scented oils, oranges, wine) under his or her nose. Sniff various parts of each other's body in natural, uninhibited way, as animals do, as if scouting each other out. Use your nose as you would use your fingers to stimulate each other and see what new sensations you can create.

Hands. Touch has been proven to have tremendous healing effects, and the role of massage is paramount in Tantra.

Here's an exercise you can use to learn how to enjoy sensations. Taking turns as giver and receiver, close your eyes and hold your partner's hand. Feel the energy of the hand you're touching and that of your own hand, so you can identify the different sensations of touching and being touched. Breathe deeply, sending energy through your hand, and explore your partner's hand. Feel the different textures (bony part, soft palm, sharp nails). Massage, using different strokes and pressures, with the intention of making your partner feel good. Give each other feedback about the different sensations of touching and being touched.

Ears. Too often neglected, this part of the body can be very erotic. Press your thumbs into the openings of the ears, pressing around the inner skin. Stretch and tug at the earlobes (they can take pressure) and around the outer ear. Whisper sweet nothings into your partner's ear. Sing a song; it doesn't matter whether you can really sing, just let yourself improvise to express yourself into your partner's ear.

You may also consider aromatherapy and the use of essential oils in your individual practices. Research has shown that such scents actually have particular effects on the brain, facilitating certain mood states.

Tantric Meditation 4

Remembering Union

This meditation also comes from the '*Vigyan Bhairav Tantra*'. Shiva says to Devi: 'Even remembering union, without embrace, the transformation happens'.

The feeling of oneness, or state of Tantric unity, is not dependent on the presence of a partner. It can be experienced alone. But it is important to have the feeling with your beloved first, and then you will be able to recall it and experience it by yourself.

For this exercise, you need to be sure that you are completely alone and will not be disturbed, otherwise you will be too self-conscious and this will prevent you from entering totally into the experience.

* Take time to prepare yourself. Have a shower, wash your hair, apply some fragrance, and wear something loose and sensual that can be easily removed. Create a sensuous atmosphere in the room.
* It will be helpful to dance, stretch and move your body for a few minutes to create a sense of physical aliveness.
* When you are ready, lie down comfortably, resting on a mattress with some cushions. Lie as if you are with your beloved. Begin to remember how it felt when you made love.
* Start to move as if you are making love with your partner. This may feel a little awkward at first, which is why it is important to be sure that you have absolute privacy. Only then can you let yourself go fully into it. Do whatever you normally do with your beloved. Move your legs, your hips, wrap your beloved in an

imaginary embrace, moan, groan, side around on the sheets. Let everything unfold as it would with your lover.

* Keep the feeling general and not located only in the sexual organs, otherwise you will feel pulled into masturbation, climax and release. This is not the point of the exercise. You are being invited to create a circle of energy within yourself, embracing both male and female qualities.
* Within a few minutes you will begin to feel this circle of energy, this union of the two opposites. You will feel both the male and female energies within yourself because in fact you have both these energies within your psyche.

As the pioneering psychologist, Carl Gustav Jung, asserted in the last century, and as Tantra has known for millennia, you have an inner man and an inner woman. They can meet, melt and merge into a circle of energy, bringing a sense of completeness and oneness.

The oneness is not just with yourself, not just with your imaginary partner. It links you with the whole cosmos, because as soon as you feel oneness you are in a state of communion with the divine. Then you will know that the other is just a door.

Sex is just a door. You can move through the door into a state of oneness with everything, which is also a state of meditation. Let this experience continue for thirty to forty minutes, or as long as it feels pleasurable, In some cases, it can continue for hours.

5

See

'The ever-present moment is the place where the whole of life unfolds — the one constant, the only reality. To see this is to wake up from Ignorance.'

Advice from a Tantric Master

One day back in 1970 a young student walked into the office of sex researcher William Hartman, MD, who was then teaching at California State University, in Long Beach, USA. This unassuming young fellow, it turned out, was a sort of philanthropist of love: he said he was able to climax again and again during a single session of lovemaking, and he was interested in teaching other men how to do it.

'At that time, we were not really aware of this phenomenon, but it piqued our interest, so we got him wired up in a laboratory,' Dr Hartman recalls. And the graphs and gauges confirmed the guy's story: Over about an hour, through masturbation, he was able to climax 16 times.

This, of course, is a bit different from most male experiences. Lots of men have learned to delay ejaculation, and occasionally may ejaculate a second time if they're able to stay aroused (and awake) long enough. But as a regular thing, one round at a time is all men are good for, seems to be the belief.

Multiple Orgasms

The two main differences between male and female orgasms, William H. Masters, MD, and Virginia E. Johnson, of the former Masters and Johnson Institute in St. Louis, point out, are that males expel seminal fluid and there's a so-called refractory period, or rest stop, after men ejaculate. Actually, the first point is wrong, but in a small way: There's increasing medical evidence that some women also ejaculate a small amount of fluid during orgasm.

Clearer to most men is that while they need a rest after climaxing, women are instantly ready for more after they orgasm. That's because women have no refractory period; a fairly high percentage of women are able to achieve their peak time after time. The female capacity for multiple orgasms far exceeds even the most prolific male. It sounds quite unbelievable but Masters and Johnson actually found women who were able to reach 50 consecutive orgasms using a vibrator.

It's these two differences — ejaculation mechanics and the need for a refractory period — that dampens a male's capacity for multiple orgasms. Or, so science once thought.

Tantra has always known differently. One key point probably discovered and rediscovered millions of times by male sexual adventurers all over the world, is this: ejaculation and orgasm are not the same thing. See this reality NOW and drop all other thoughts and beliefs about this subject.

It's now widely acknowledged that there is a difference between the pleasurable sensations of orgasm and the physical event of ejaculation. You can have an orgasm without ejaculating, and you can ejaculate without having an orgasm. Which means that your capacity to repeatedly reach orgasm is not limited by your capacity to repeatedly ejaculate (which is fairly limited).

This is one of the sexual secrets multi-orgasmic men have learned: to detach orgasm from ejaculation. Essentially, they've learned to take themselves to the brink of ejaculation, then stop and relax, allowing the rush of orgasm to sweep over them; then they do it again.

The orgasmic pattern in men seems to vary, according to the few studies that have been conducted on the subject. These men may have a series of 'dry' orgasms, without ejaculating at all, then ejaculate explosively; they may ejaculate in a series, releasing an increasingly smaller amount of ejaculate each time; or in some other pattern. But they're always able to distinguish between the two.

The second point, that men need a refractory period after orgasm, also has its exceptions, it turns out. The physiological purpose of the refractory period is not entirely clear, Dr Hartman admits. Once you've ejaculated, it certainly takes a certain amount of time for the prostate, seminal vesicles and other ducts to refill with fluid. But to fully refill these ducts takes hours, sometimes even overnight; the refractory period is far shorter, suggesting it is not merely a break for refilling.

Some men seem to have only a brief or partial refractory period, Dr Hartman points out. These guys often don't lose their erections before they rise to the occasion a second, third or fourth time. 'Their heart rates (a key indicator of orgasm) may top out at 150 during orgasm, but they never fall back to a resting state of, say, 70; they drop back to 120, then bounce right back up to 150 when they have another orgasm', he says.

All Men Can

Inspired by his first subject, Dr Hartman eventually located 32 other multi-orgasmic males. For the benefit of science these men agreed to repeatedly bring themselves to orgasm by hand, in a small, dimly lit room in a laboratory, while wired up to a heart monitor and other devices. In 1984, he and his wife, Marian, co-directors of the Centre for Marital and Sexual Studies in Long Beach, California, published a book called *Any man Can*. It reported their laboratory findings about these remarkable men and described the simple techniques by which, they claimed, any man can learn to become multi-orgasmic.

What was it, exactly, that they were practising? Dr Hartman says it boils down to three simple techniques. It's interesting to note that all three of these techniques were being practised thousands of years earlier by the Tantrics in India and the Taoists in China (these techniques will develop in greater detail as we move further into the book).

Technique 1 — The Stop-Start or Squeeze Technique. Back in 1955, a urologist at Duke University Medical School in Durham, North Carolina, named James Semans, MD, described a technique for treating premature ejaculation that he originally learned from a prostitute-turned-sexual-surrogate. Over the years it has proven so effective that it's now used by sex therapists all over the country as a way of teaching ejaculatory control.

Basically, you simply masturbate to the brink of ejaculation, then stop; do it again, then stop until your body learns to gain control over what is wrongly perceived as one of the most uncontrollable of impulses. Eventually, with any luck you'll begin to have the amazing experience of reaching orgasm without ejaculating.

Some therapists recommend that you squeeze the tip of the penis tightly just before ejaculation, with two fingers underneath and the thumb on top. This method is called the squeeze technique. But other therapists say simply stopping, then starting again (the stop-start technique) works just as well.

First, lay on your back while doing this, to get used to the female-superior position during intercourse (most multi-orgasmic males prefer the female-on-top position). Using a light touch, stimulate yourself right up to near ejaculation, then squeeze or stop, Hold still for 15 or 20 seconds (not too long), until the urge to ejaculate begins to ebb. Then start again. Learn to bring yourself to the brink of ejaculation three or four times before letting go. You can do this same drill with a partner; just get her to squeeze or stop.

'We've found that learning the squeeze technique is the quickest way for men to become multi-orgasmic,' Dr Hartman says. 'Many men can achieve adequate control through the squeeze method in a couple of weeks'.

Most therapists recommend that while you're learning this technique, you abstain from other kinds of masturbation or intercourse. You're trying to re-train your body, and reverting to the old way will erase your newfound gains. Also, you should practice for several weeks, three to five times a week.

Technique 2 — Kegel Exercises. A group of deep pelvic muscles called the pubococcygeus, or PC muscles, are known to have a profound effect on men's and women's enjoyment of sex. The PC muscles, which are slung between your legs to provide a sort of floor for the pelvis, are the same muscles you use to shut off the flow of urine in mid-stream. So that's your first task: get acquainted with your PC muscles by shutting off the flow of urine. That squeezing, sometimes called a pelvic quickie, is better known as a Kegel exercise, after the gynaecologist who began teaching them to women with stress incontinence back in the 1950s. Squeeze often during the day, everyday, with the goal of truly strengthening the muscles. The great thing about Kegel exercises is that no one ever knows you are doing them.

Technique 3 — Keep Your Testicles Down. You've probably never noticed this before, but just before ejaculation, your usually pendulous testicles raise up very close to body, like a pair of helium balloons floating up to the ceiling. 'The phenomenon of testicular elevation is of extreme physiological importance,' Masters and Johnson reported. 'If the testes do not undergo at least partial elevation, the human male will not experience a full ejaculatory sequence.'

So multi-orgasmic men have learned to keep their testicles pulled down to delay ejaculation, either by holding them between their legs or by gently tugging them down with one hand (or getting her to tug them down).

Being able to climax more than once is potentially a more useful and interesting skill than being good around the house. It's however a big mistake to set it up as just another desperate male goal, another target to achieve during lovemaking. **Tantrics have always believed the end product of lovemaking is intimacy, not orgasm.** I want you to see this reality too.

It's like income: if you focus on money, you never make enough, and if you focus on orgasms, you never have enough. The goal of lovemaking is to become intimate with another person.

Prolonging your Lovemaking

Sexually, men face two major difficulties throughout their lives. The first is as a young, virile teenager being unable to last long enough to satisfy a woman, or even satisfy yourself. After weeks of anticipation it is often all over in a few minutes. Do you remember those times? Or are you still in the position of sometimes not lasting as long as you would like? What an embarrassment it is for a man of any age to ejaculate too soon. Not a happy memory at all.

Not a happy memory for a married man either, especially if your wife does not want sex as much as you do. When she does, you ejaculate too soon and she is left feeling frustrated and sometimes angry. Even though she might not say so or show it, she feels it. Not good times for a man of any age.

Be honest about this. If it is a problem sometimes and you want to do something about it, the first step is to acknowledge it to yourself. Remember, you are not the only man who faces this difficulty.

The second major difficulty it is that, at some stage in your later years, you will no longer come too soon — you won't come at all. You won't be able to get an erection or, if you do, it certainly won't stand up as straight and hard as it used to. Very often your woman's sexual energy has increased, because most women reach their sexual prime when they are around forty. There is the opportunity for sex but you can't do anything about it because your sexual energy is not as strong. If you do get an erection and ejaculate, instead of the mind-blowing explosion it used to be, it is more like a squeak than a roar.

However, there is something you can do about it, as this loss of function is not necessarily a part of ageing. These major difficulties can be overcome through learning the essential techniques of ejaculation control.

Any man with the desire and persistence to practice can develop himself this way, no matter what his age. Although different problems occur at different ages in life, the techniques achieve the same results — an experience of better lovemaking than you ever dreamed possible. The strength of your erection and your ability to last as long as you want without ejaculation is not all that lovemaking is about. This skill alone does not guarantee you'll be a success in bed. With lovemaking it's not only skill with your sexual techniques but skill with your heart that makes you a good lover.

Men who are able to feel their love and share these deep feelings will never have a shortage of women in their lives. **The ability to feel love and intimacy and to be able to express these feelings with sensitivity and passion is also what being a good lover is about.** To become an enlightened lover, it is essential that you see this as a reality.

A lot of people use the term making love to describe the art of having sex, but to me making love is quite different. When you are not in a loving relationship and you are having sex purely for the physical pleasure it gives, I call that sex. It doesn't mean that you don't care for, respect and nurture each other, but it isn't the kind of love you can have for someone with whom you are in a deep relationship. Lovemaking is quite unique, a blending of your sexual passion — the heat in your genitals — with the deep love and intimacy you feel in your heart.

In a loving relationship it's a real awakening to conscientiously stop in the middle of lovemaking and ask yourself: 'How much love am I feeling right now?' and to be aware throughout your lovemaking of how much love you are actually feeling, as opposed to how long you can last. Usually your mind is preoccupied with how much longer you can go before ejaculating. 'I wish she'd come. I can't last much longer! God, it feels so good! Oh no, I'm coming' thoughts like these are common for many men.

Most men who are open to learning about lovemaking realize that a woman's sexual energy takes longer to warm than man's sexual energy. The Taoist Chinese tradition refers to a man's sexual energy as being that of fire, while woman's sexual energy is that of water. When fire and water get together the fire goes out and this is what happens in lovemaking. If there's no education the fire goes out — the man ejaculates and the water is barely warmed. With skill, the man's fire can warm the woman's water through the techniques of ejaculation control.

A man needs to be able to last long enough to warm the water to a state of climax to satisfy the woman.

The Importance of Controlling Ejaculation

Techniques for ejaculation control are described in great detail in Taoist and Tantric texts from ancient China and India, respectively. Although the information is fantastic, it is often so complicated with detail and with Chinese terminology or Hindu methodology that it is difficult to read and understand.

My intention is to keep techniques and terms as simple as I can so that the practice becomes more important than the understanding of terminology. However, as simplified as I can make them, I don't want to mislead you into believing that these lovemaking skills will work for you the first time you try them. As with learning any other skill, you need to practice each one before you can do it easily. In the early stages your mind might be focused on getting it right, but once you master the practices, things flow, just like learning to dance. It's a mind and body skill, not just mental concentration or willpower.

Some of you will try these techniques and get immediate results, especially those of you who have some understanding of working with energy in your body through yoga, t'ai chi, massage, or dance. To master the skills takes some training. Its common sense that if you practice something regularly you will get better at it more quickly.

You have probably placed lovemaking high on the list of things you can enjoy, so it's worth spending the time to master these techniques. The value will be enormous because lovemaking is something you'll be doing regularly throughout your life, whenever you are in a relationship. So the time you spend now developing these skills will benefit you for the rest of your life.

As a man it will always make you feel good to know that during lovemaking you can let go with your pleasure, your joy, your excitement — any time the energy takes you — and still last as long as you want.

The key is control, not tension. The word control often implies tension — fighting against something — but this is not the type of control I'm talking about developing. With these techniques I want to focus on working in a relaxed state, a manner of control like meditation.

You can be in control in such a way that it's not a fight; rather, you're totally flowing with the energy — centred, experiencing everything that is happening. When you are learning to dance you are very much in control and there's a certain rigidity to your movement because you concentrate closely on every step you make. Once you have mastered the steps, although you are in control you can move more freely to the music. It takes a lot of training to achieve the end result.

Some of that training can be done separate from lovemaking. A tennis player in training will practice certain strokes over and over again, then when he's playing a match he doesn't think about the strokes or the practice. Because of the training the stroke becomes automatic. If your partner wants to help you with the training while making love, then that is ideal. You become teammates in the game of love, with the goal being more pleasure for both of you. It's a good game to play!

Learning to be a good lover is essential, so that when you meet a woman with whom you want to form a relationship you will be far ahead of the lover who enters and literally blows it the first time. Single men spend a lot of time looking for the right woman. When and if you find her you'll need to have something special to offer her.

Having a good lover is incredibly important to most women. Whether they admit it or not, every woman would love to have fabulous, orgasmic sex and feel loved. According to some research, some men ejaculate within three to five minutes of movement within a woman. You can't create a heightened sexual experience for her in three to five minutes! If you have the ability to be there with her totally as long as she wants, feeling the love instead of having to concentrate on facilitating orgasm or not coming too soon, she will think you're divine.

Ejaculation control will help create longer lovemaking sessions where you will be able to give and receive much more love. It will help you to reach a stage where there isn't any line between loving, touching and actually making love.

This is what every woman wants, and you can achieve this when you master these techniques.

Secret 1 — The PC Muscle

You will find this technique coming up again and again throughout this book. It is one of the foundation practices of becoming a Tantric lover. So practice it repeatedly. You will be amazed by the powerful benefits you receive in a short time.

The first and most important thing to learn in mastering these lovemaking techniques is how to strengthen your pubococcygeus muscle, the 'love muscle'. This is the major muscle of contraction in male and female orgasm. Strengthening the PC muscle helps to strengthen your erection and increase the sensations of your climax, which is very important in older years.

The PC muscle extends from the base of the spine, where it is connected to the tailbone (the coccyx), to the front of the body, where it is connected to the pubic bone. It is the PC muscle you use to cut off urination in mid-stream. Just as you can tense and release your fist or tense and release your shoulders, you can tense and release the PC muscle. This will exercise the muscle involved in sexual pleasure.

Try it out now to give yourself the idea of what I'm writing about here. Tense your fist and feel your biceps muscle tighten, then release — totally. Now see if you can tense and release the biceps muscle alone.

Muscle isolation practice will help you to isolate the PC muscle.

The next time you urinate, try to stop the flow in mid-stream to get a feeling of isolating and activating the PC muscle. At first you may need to tighten the whole pelvic floor, which includes the anus muscle and perhaps the lower abdominal muscles. Some men may need to sense the whole upper body to pull up the PC muscle.

See if you can locate the PC muscle. Flex it, even if your whole body tightens. Just as you isolated the muscle in the biceps from the fist, you can totally relax your upper body and still tense the pelvic floor.

Try it now as you are reading this. Your pelvic floor is tight but the rest of your body is relaxed. As you practice this regularly and your PC muscle gets stronger, you will be able to distinguish it from the nearby muscles. In the earlier stages do not concern yourself with this — just tighten and release all the muscles in this pelvic floor area, including the anus and buttocks. Continue to tighten and release several times.

Later, stand in front of a mirror and continually draw up and release this PC muscle, as if you are holding back urination. You will notice that you can make the lingam (penis) move up and down as you tighten and release this muscle. If you can do this, then you know you are exercising the right muscle.

Now that you have located this muscle you can begin to strengthen it. Incorporate these simple exercises into your daily routine, independent of your lovemaking sessions. Then the exercises will become habitual and you won't have to set aside a special time to practice. For example, you can practice while you travel to and from work. No one will know what you are doing.

Strengthening the PC muscle is one of the greatest sexual secrets a man can know.

You can strengthen this muscle with the following exercises:

The PC Hold. Contract the PC muscle as if you were holding back urination in midstream. Hold it and count to three, then release. Make sure the muscle completely relaxes before your next contraction. Hold it again, then release.

Draw it up now while you are reading this book. Hold count to three and release. Do this at least twenty times in your first session. You can build up to whatever number of repetitions is comfortable for you. I suggest you commit yourself to five minutes on the way to work and five minutes while travelling home.

You can practice this exercise while you are sitting or standing, walking or resting. It may assist you if you combine it with the breath. Breathe in as you contract a muscle. Hold your breath and the contraction for a count of three. And then make an extra strong contraction. Now release the muscle and the breath together. Do twenty cycles at a time. If after a week of practice you experience any soreness, take it easy. The pubococcygeus is like any other muscle if you overdo it in the early stages, it can become tender.

Fluttering the PC. Start this exercise by contracting the PC muscle. Tighten the muscle with a squeeze contraction, hold momentarily, then release completely. Squeeze, hold and release while breathing normally. Concentrate on each contraction as you do it. The contractions are as strong as before, but they are made approximately one per second, like a heartbeat. As you get better try fluttering the muscle at approximately four contractions per second and then much faster. I think of a butterfly's wings fluttering. You can feel the penis, the lingam, moving up and down. Complete three cycles of twenty contractions.

Incorporate these exercises into your daily routine, or do the one you find easier. Practice every day, with normal breathing. Make sure you relax the muscles between contractions — this is very important. Relaxing pelvic floor and buttock muscles during lovemaking is crucial to lasting longer. As the PC muscle gets stronger it's simple to gently spread the energy out of the genitals during intercourse and the urgency to ejaculate passes.

It is believed that ancient Indian emperors had Tantric sages train their sons in these techniques. To test if the sage was proficient enough to teach the son, the sage would need to be able to place his penis in a bowl of water and, using the PC muscle, sip the water through the penis until the bowl was emptied. The more proficient teachers could do it with oil. Such a person would obviously have no trouble with ejaculation control.

It is important to understand the potential strength of the PC muscle in men. If your job involves sitting for long stretches of time without movement in the pelvic region, the muscles can become very weak over the years. People in these jobs are more susceptible to prostate trouble and may experience difficulty around the age of forty and sometimes earlier. If you work in one of these jobs but have sex a lot, you will be getting some exercise in this muscle, because it's often only when we are making love that this area of the body gets exercised.

So if you have a job that involves a lot of sitting, you may need to compensate by making love at least twice a day! (Hey, that was just a joke, Tantric teaching should be fun). If you are involved in a sedentary job, compensate by practising the exercise above at least twice a day with disciplined dedication.

Learning to Receive. You need to be careful during lovemaking that you are not just performing to get a result. Men often find themselves doing that because they have been conditioned by a society that pushes for results or by parents who gave love and attention only for winning, for getting a result.

Most men live their lives like this, until they become aware that they are so busy performing and producing results that they have forgotten how to receive love and nurture themselves.

In lovemaking men forget to receive the gift of love and healing energy their partners are giving. Men are often so busy trying to get a result that they miss the experience. Magazines and other media have put men under so much pressure to produce — to be good providers, good lovers, to bring their women to orgasm that now they are very often in the position of being unfulfiled themselves in their lovemaking.

It's not just about giving your woman more pleasure; it's also about receiving more pleasure. If your woman realizes you are receiving a lot of pleasure from making love with her, then that also gives her pleasure.

Secret 2 — Control of Breath

What most men do as excitement builds up and they get close to the climax is move harder and faster and breathe heavier and faster, or else they hold the breath. If we are to reverse the flow of sexual energy, the best way to do it is to breathe slowly and deeply and rhythmically. Even if you do move rapidly and your partner is moving fast too, keep your breaths long, deep and consistent. Breathing does not have to match your movements. As you breathe in, imagine breathing in all the love essences, the scent, the beautiful sensations, and the images of your lover's body. Drink deeply of every magical moment of your lovemaking; do not miss one minute of this experience.

Here is a helpful exercise you can practice separate from lovemaking. It's an excellent meditation for single men to practice. This exercise is an advanced technique of breath and PC muscle control, using the PC strengthening techniques discussed earlier.

Merging the Breath and the PC. You should preferably sit in a chair for this exercise. Imagine the opening of your lingam is like a straw. Engage the PC muscle and 'sip' energy up through your penis the way you would sip liquid through a straw. Make a soft sipping sound to assist you as you practice.

Imagine that nectar is being drawn up through you lingam, right up the spine to the base of your neck, right up to the top of your head. Now lock that energy in by pulling your chin into your chest and stretching the back of your neck. With your back straight, hold the energy for a few seconds. Then release the chin and the breath while making the sound 'aahhh.' Bear down on the PC muscle and release it as you let the breath go.

Repeat the exercise as many times as you can.

It is important that you actually feel the energy rise and fall and not just visualize it. This process can last for a period of five minutes. It's a good idea to try out this practice on your morning erections to test if you really can do it and that it's not just your imagination. See how many contractions it takes for you to make your penis go soft.

If you practice yoga you may prefer to sit in the cross-legged position. Yogis often do this exercise with their legs crossed so that one heel presses on the PC area. Some people do it sitting on a tennis ball or something similar that presses on the PC area.

If you feel a little dizzy afterward (because you are actually drawing energy up into your head), then try taking the energy up only as high as the throat, swallow; then breathe out as you feel the energy going down again.

Rub your belly strongly after the exercise, 81 times clockwise and 81 times counterclockwise, to spread the energy through your body. If you continue to experience dizziness during the exercise, then contract the PC muscle as you breathe in and out: but do not sip the energy up to the crown. As you release the PC muscle and breathe out, feel the energy spread throughout your body.

Similar exercises are done by women to assist in childbirth — for them it's important not to take the energy to the head, but simply to squeeze and release the PC muscle. Coordination of the PC muscle and breath is excellent training for lovemaking, the kind of lovemaking where you have control over your ejaculation.

Secret 3 — Release Muscle Tension

The muscles of a man's body are conditioned to respond in a certain way as he builds toward ejaculation. They help him to ejaculate quickly. How did this happen? It's certainly not what a man wants to happen when he is with a woman!

These muscles probably were conditioned at puberty. Young boys like the sensation of ejaculation and so they masturbate like crazy to get that feeling as quickly as possible. As they begin courting girls, sex is often in limited supply, so when they get the chance they go for it. Very often there is a lot of tension when adolescent lovemaking doesn't happen in a safe and private place. Afraid that someone will see them, teenagers try to get it over with quickly.

Even though, on a conscious level, we want to last longer with our women, our bodies have learned to come more quickly. So we need to reprogram what the muscles do as we are approaching climax. We need to learn how to relax the muscles as they begin to tense. The subconscious mind is also conditioned to climax quickly because sex is often associated with secrecy and guilt.

Subconsciously it's best to get it over swiftly because we don't want to feel guilty for too long. Even if as sexually educated men we may know it's necessary for our women's pleasure for us to last longer, our bodies, our muscular systems, and our subconscious minds already have been programmed to climax quickly. Without training the subconscious is more powerful than the conscious mind.

Do you know what happens with your body's responses and your thoughts as you are nearing climax? Because your body is conditioned to climax quickly, the muscles necessary to cause this will automatically start to contract. Your breath will do what is necessary to assist you in climaxing quickly. Your mind will become stressed and your thoughts frantic as you fight the urge, especially when you know your woman would like to go on much longer.

However, if you can observe your conditioned response you can also work at reversing the conditioning. It's not difficult — it's just a matter of awareness and a little training. Biofeedback works on the same principle. If, for example, you are suffering from stress, you can be linked to biofeedback machines and learn to find trigger points to release certain muscles before they tense any further. It works very effectively.

The best way to do it is while masturbating. Think of it as a self-pleasuring experiment to derive some invaluable feedback on yourself. If you are a single person and masturbate regularly, this self-pleasuring experiment won't be any problem for you. However, I know that many men in steady sexual relationships will not have masturbated for years, and you may experience some initial resistance.

Ejaculation and Orgasms

One of the best-kept secrets of our time is that men (not just women) can be multi-orgasmic. Not only can a man have several orgasms during one session of lovemaking, but he also can do it and still have lots of energy and desire. 'Oh sure,' you may be thinking, 'maybe some super stud, but not me.' Actually most men can, you can — the key is learning to separate orgasm from ejaculation. Because ejaculation follows orgasm so closely — within a split second — most people think they are one and the same, but they are two distinct phenomena.

In Tantric loving, you will learn to experience the pleasure of orgasm without the accompanying let-down of ejaculation. There are only two things you need to learn in order to be able to separate your orgasm from your ejaculation:

* Stay relaxed no matter how aroused you are.
* Move your hot sexual energy up and away from your genitals.

Any man who does this and makes love long enough to build a very high sexual charge will eventually spontaneously experience non-ejaculatory orgasm.

A man is known to experience three different kinds of orgasms in his lovemaking, and can actually learn to master them at will:

The Ejaculatory Orgasm

Most men are happily familiar with a regular ejaculatory orgasm during which the whole body tenses, and the prostate gland vibrates strongly propelling semen forcefully out of the penis. For a few seconds there is intense pleasure, and then a refractory (or recovery) period sets in. The body relaxes; the erection subsides and with it goes interest in further sexual activity. Sleepiness sets in. How long it takes before energy and interest return depends on a man's age, health, libido, and frequency of ejaculation. Some men, usually young and strong men, may be able to retain an erection in spite of ejaculation by continued thrusting, or they may gain another erection almost immediately.

No matter how good it feels, repeated ejaculation with its accompanying loss of sexual energy can deplete your body's strength and vitality. If the energy drain is extensive, it can lead to unconscious resentment of your partner for 'exhausting your manhood'.

The Prostate Orgasm

Although the prostate orgasm is also accompanied by ejaculation, less fluid is expelled. Because the contractions of the prostate are much less powerful, the ejaculate dribbles out and pleasurable sensations are felt more internally. The usual tiredness following orgasm is noticeably reduced. Some men experience prostate orgasm occasionally and unexpectedly. For those practising the art of Tantric loving, it is a sign that you are learning to keep the muscles around your genitals relaxed even during high arousal and vigorous activity. It is a step along your road to mastery.

The Non-Ejaculatory Orgasm

By building a high sexual charge and moving it up through your body rather than releasing it through ejaculation, you can discover non-ejaculatory orgasm. Your whole body can become an orgasmic erogenous zone, with orgasmic sensation in your toes, for example, or intense orgasmic rippling through your entire body rather than just your genitals.

There are no limits to how many of these orgasms you can have, with the intensity of each one varying from mild to overwhelming. A non-ejaculatory orgasm does not result in any loss of energy. On the contrary, your energy can build indefinitely to higher and higher intensities. You may experience the opening of your higher spiritual centres, specifically your throat, third eye, and crown chakra energy centres. Furthermore, you can build up reserves of sexual energy and use it for other purposes, much as physical healing, spiritual awakening, enhanced creativity, or excellence in science, business, and sports. Any man who learns to do this will gain a serious competitive advantage.

A non-ejaculatory orgasm usually feels different from a regular ejaculatory orgasm, although sometimes the sensations that accompany a normal ejaculation are also experienced. That familiar intense pleasure that starts in the vibrating prostate and typically travels out the end of the penis with the ejaculate instead travels upward along the energy meridians of the chakra centres to the top of your head, As this energy moves, you may experience intense sensations of pleasure throughout your body. These sensations are not the same as the sensation located in the genitals during ordinary orgasm, but they are superb. My body often contracts and jerks involuntarily with the force of this flow of energy. This rush of sensations lasts much longer than a genital orgasm, from several minutes up to a timeless, continuous bliss state.

Mastering your Ejaculation

A wise Tantric master once said, 'The archer strikes the target — partly by pulling; partly by letting go.'

With regular lovemaking, there is a steady build-up of sexual excitement to ejaculatory orgasmic release, which usually ends the sexual activity. Tantric sacred sex is high-energy sex. You make love for a period of hours, building higher and higher concentrations of energy, stopping before you let go into ejaculation, relaxing a little, then building excitement again and again. By delaying ejaculation, you accumulate enough sexual energy to open your spiritual centres, plus you last long enough so your lover may experience multiple orgasms. But don't make the mistake of putting all your effort and attention into simply preventing ejaculation. When your focus is on not ejaculating, your mind is still locked on ejaculation. This consciousness only notices the object of your attention. If you focus on 'I do not want to ejaculate,' the object of your attention is ejaculation, and you are going to get more of that. Instead, your effort should be positive, on learning to accumulate and then circulate more and more sexual energy. Using your imagination to think about and visualize working with your sexual energy is one of the positive methods you can use to replace the negative idea of not ejaculating.

Secrets to Delaying your Pleasure

You will soon find that mapping your arousal scale and identifying your signals at the points of no return is the easy part. What is much more challenging is making the choice to do something about it. The urge to go on to ejaculation may be overwhelming — like trying to stop a team of wild horses. However, if you do want to make that next step toward ecstasy, for yourself and your partner, here are some simple hints.

1. Stop. Stop whatever you were doing to build your sexual excitement and become still. This is almost guaranteed to work unless you have waited too long and ejaculation has already started. If necessary, you can interrupt intercourse — as you gain mastery it may be sufficient only to slow down without actually coming to a complete stop. Wait for the excitement to subside and your sexual energy to become more manageable before resuming active intercourse, oral sex, or manual stimulation.

2. Breathe. Just as rapid breathing helps to build your excitement and effectively indicates how aroused you are, slow, deep breathing calms and relaxes you. By paying very close attention to your breath, you are also taking your attention away from your genitals, so your urge to ejaculate lessens.

3. Sounds. You may have noticed that when martial artists are making a hit, they often give a loud yell. The sound carries their energy with it. You can use sound to circulate your sexual energy up out of your genitals and through the rest of your body. It really does not make much difference what sounds you make. Experiment — yell, scream, make animal sounds, talk into each other's ears, say or sing words of love and adoration. Talk wildly and lewdly when the level of excitement and passion builds to the right fever pitch. If you are used to being quiet when you make love and you want to add in some sound effects, you may wish to alert your partner beforehand. I highly recommend that you both make noise while you make love. The more noise you make, the better. Besides moving energy, it gives your partner feedback about what you like and do not like, and your rising level of excitement.

4. Testes Tug. Because a man's scrotum pulls up tight to his body just before ejaculation, an effective delaying action is to gently tug the testes down periodically during lovemaking. You can do this yourself or your partner can do the honours with hands or mouth, pulling gently or more firmly according to your preference.

5. Penis tip Squeeze. This technique works best with masturbation or manual or oral stimulation by a partner and is especially effective during your early days of learning. It can be used in conjunction with intercourse, but requires complete withdrawal. At the height of your erection, firmly grasp the tip of the penis in one hand so that the palm of your hand closes over the tip of the penis. Do not try this if ejaculation has already started — it will be ineffective and painful. Combine this technique with applying pressure at the base of the penis where the shaft rises out of the pubic bone. One hand presses against the pubic bone, with the thumb on one side and the first two fingers on the other side of the shaft, while the other hand squeezes the tip of the penis.

6. Wear a Condom. Experiment with wearing a condom, not only for the purpose of safe sex, but also to decrease the sensitivity of your penis. This may make quite a bit of difference in how long you can maintain your erection.

7. Focus on your Partner. Train your mind to think of something other than ejaculation. I do not recommend reciting sports statistics, talking about a movie, or in any way diverting your attention from lovemaking. It is essential that you be fully present from moment to moment. However, instead of thinking about ejaculation, or worrying about ejaculating too quickly, I suggest you think about pleasing your partner.

Learn to take pleasure for yourself by pleasing her. Notice how she reacts when your tongue is exploring around her clitoris, but also notice how her clitoris feels on your tongue. Notice how she enjoys when you suck on her nipples, but also notice how her breasts feel pressed against your face. Notice how she moans when you gently run your fingers up the inside of her thighs, but also notice how her skin feels so soft and warm against your fingers. Keep your attention on your partner, not on yourself!

8. Affirmations. Using affirmations before, during, or after lovemaking can help your staying power.

Affirmations are a form of communication between your conscious and subconscious layers of mind. But not all affirmations are equal, many are a disguised form of lying to yourself. For example, if you ejaculate prematurely and you say to yourself as an affirmation, ' I can last for hours without ejaculation,' you are lying to yourself, which will cause inner resistance and stress. Better to select words that state the possibility of doing what you want to be able to do. For example, you might rephrase the ejaculation affirmation in any of the following ways: 'I am learning to master delaying ejaculation.' 'With practice I will become a master at being able to delay ejaculation.' 'Learning to delay ejaculation is fun and easy.' Make sure any statement is true. Do not add words such as 'fun' and 'easy' if they are not true.

There is a great scene in the popular movie The Matrix, where the hero is being taken to meet the oracle to try to determine if he is 'the one' chosen to defeat The Matrix. He is ushered into a waiting room with many bending and twisting it with his mind. Our hero stoops down in astonishment at this phenomenon. He takes the spoon from the boy and tries to bend it with his mind.

The boy speaks: 'Do not try and bend the spoon; that's impossible. Instead, only try to realize the truth.'

'What is that?' asks our hero.

'There is no spoon.'

'There is no spoon?' echoes the hero.

'Then you'll see that it is not the spoon that bends, it is only yourself.'

This is an illustration of union of all that was formerly separate. This is the same state that is the culmination of Tantra, the joining of the lovers and God — the healing of separation. In this state, there is no controlling of ejaculation, no ejaculation mastery; rather, there is a state of high *satori or samadhi*. This culmination is not the result of any effort you have made to learn about delaying ejaculation, but it does follow that effort.

Experiencing this is not an accomplishment, but rather a gift.

2 Yogic Aids in Prolonging Pleasure

The path to psychosexual power begins not only with recognizing and overcoming restrictive sexual prejudices, but also with cultivating intense gonadal awareness through conscious tightening of the pelvic floor. This is accomplished through deliberate, selective contraction and relaxation of the anal and urethral (urinary) sphincters.

These exercises have been traditional for thousands of years in Tantra Yoga and throughout Asia. As I mentioned earlier, the techniques have been re-discovered by Western gynaecologists and sex therapists such as Dr Kegel and Drs Masters and Johnson. We should remember that the word 'discover' etymologically means to 'uncover', so in actuality there is nothing new under the sun. The encounter movement in psychology still has much to rediscover or uncover from Tantra in regard to touch therapy.

The Mula-Bandha. This is a perineum or pelvic contraction lock which begins at the anal sphincter and spreads forward to the genitals.

Key: the correct feeling of anal locking may be understood by recalling the sensation induced by holding back the passage of stool from the bowel.

Method

* Sit erect in any comfortable position, hands palm up on the thighs.
* Focus attention on the anal region, beginning with awareness of the floor or chair exerting pressure up against the buttocks and then pinpoint consciousness upon the anus.
* Inhale a half-lungful of air, swallow and retain breath.
* Slowly contract the anus to maximum while continuing to hold the breath. Breath is retained throughout up to step six.
* Women: spread pelvic floor contraction forward from the anus until a distinct twitch is felt in the vaginal lips. Men: spread pelvic floor contraction forward from the anus until distinct pull is felt upon testicles resting in scrotal sac.
* Release pelvic contraction completely, take in a sniff of fresh air and then smoothly exhale fully.

Advantages of Mula Bandha

* Tones the anal sphincters, preventing and curing (in early stages) haemorrhoids and anal pruritus.
* Sends a blood flush stimulating the uro-genital system in both men and women.

* In women: tightens slack vaginal walls and reduces tendency toward so-called frigidity or orgasmic impairment. In men: reduces tendency for premature ejaculation and impotence.
* Awakens *Muladhara* Chakra.

The Vajroli-Mudra. This is a simplified form of the classical *Vajroli Mudra* revealed to the Western world by Indian yogis.

Key: Vajroli Mudra involves urethral sphincter closure exactly when you cut off the flow of urine in midstream while voiding.

Preliminary awareness training: drink several pints of water on an empty stomach. In an hour, empty the bladder. Practice cutting off and restarting the urine flow at least a dozen times until the bladder is fully drained.

Method

* Sit erect in any comfortable position, hands palm up on the thighs.
* Focus attention on the urethral sphincter, below the clitoris in women and at the base of the penis (near the pubic bone) in men.
* Inhale a half — lungful of air, swallow and retain the breath.
* Contract urethral orifice exactly as when cutting off urine flow and at the same time pull up the lower abdomen as if attempting to suck genitals into the pelvis. Relax the contraction and repeat as many times as possible on that breath, allowing a feeling of sexual excitement to spread up the spinal cord from the pelvis to the brain.
* Cease the contractions, relax the abdomen, take in a sniff of fresh air and then smoothly exhale fully.

Auxiliary check exercise: Women: gently insert one or two fingers in the vagina and perform *Vajroli Mudra*. When done correctly contractions should spread, causing the vagina to clasp the fingers gently. *Men:* perform *Vajroli Mudra* standing naked in front of the mirror. Watch to check that the head of the penis twitches or elevates slightly with each contraction.

Advantages of *Vajroli Mudra*

* Tones urethral sphincter, preventing and curing (in early stages) urinary stress incontinence.
* Sends blood flush stimulating uro-genital system in both men and women.
* Women: encourages clitoral sensitivity. Men: encourages erectile potency.
* Awakens *Swadhisthana* Chakra.

Accomplished yoga masters advise that the *Mula Bandha* should be followed by *Vajroli Mudra* daily, beginning with ten repetitions of each, adding five additional repetitions a week until a maximum of sixty rounds each is performed a day. One round equals completion from the first step to last.

Note that some people will achieve better control with three-quarters of lungful of air or even full lungs rather than with the suggested half-breath. The sniff of air in the final step of each exercise is a *pranayama* device designed to give instant relief after *Kumbhaka* (breath retention) and permit a controlled, full exhalation.

Mula Bandha and *Vajroli Mudra* develop pelvic thrust ability in the male and penile gripping power in the female, enhancing sensitivity and control during intercourse for both sexes.

Understand that Ejaculation and Orgasm Are Different

The relationship between ejaculation and orgasm is crucial to how long a man lasts in sex. Read the following two statements and circle whether you think they are true or false:

* True or false? A man can ejaculate without experiencing an orgasm.
* True or false? A man can have an orgasm without ejaculating.

Both are true. Understanding that ejaculation and orgasm are two separate functions is crucial to the delights of Tantric sex. A man can delay ejaculation or not ejaculate at all, but still achieve orgasm and not just one orgasm, but many. Men can have multiple orgasms, just like women, To understand this, one has to understand the physiology of the man's body.

The mechanism of ejaculation, like an erection reflex, is triggered from the spinal cord (the sympathetic nervous system). The penis responds to stimulation by sending a message to the lumbar portion of the spinal cord (the ejaculatory centre) through the nerves. This triggers contractions of muscles in the internal genital organs. Although, it all sounds so automatic, the timing of the process can actually be controlled consciously.

Traditional Control Tactics

Once again, to refresh your memory, remember that some of the traditional ways to help man overcome premature ejaculation have included the following techniques:

Stop-start. This technique was popularized by the famous sex therapist and research team of Masters and Johnson more than 40 years ago, but is still effective. The man stimulates himself to the point where he feels he will ejaculate and then stops the stimulation. When he feels more in control, he starts stimulation again.

Squeeze. When he feels the urge to ejaculate, he applies pressure on the shaft of the lingam, where the shaft connects to the head, with the thumb on the top and the forefinger and middle finger on the underside, on either side of the bump that is sensitive (the frenulum). When the urge subsides, he resumes stimulation.

The testicle tug. At the point of no return the man pulls his testicles down (gently) to inhibit the ejaculation. This method is tricky and potentially dangerous (don't pull too hard), so try the others first, please.

The man can do these techniques on his own or his partner can help. It's best if he learns on his own what works best for him and then teaches her. Give her precise cues (sounds, movements) about what to do.

Tantric Sex vs Other Methods of Prolonging Lovemaking

Of course, you can delay ejaculation through these traditional sex therapy methods — sex therapists have been teaching certain ejaculation delay methods for decades, since Masters and Johnson re-framed and popularized them more than 40 years ago. The stop-start and squeeze techniques are effective; however, they can be even more effective when you add techniques of Tantric sexuality while carrying them out.

The secret is to encourage the man to focus on, direct and channel his sexual energy.

Conscious awareness of sexual energy when performing any of the traditional methods of ejaculatory control is important in Tantric practice and makes the man and his partner more attuned to his body's needs and responses.

The table on page 144 summarizes the several differences between traditional sex therapy techniques for premature ejaculation and Tantric sex techniques.

There are also similarities between traditional sex therapy techniques and Tantric sex techniques. Both —

* Emphasize relaxation.
* Focus on enjoying sensations in all parts of the body (called sensate focus in traditional sex therapy).
* Recommended practices for the limp lingam, such as stuffing in traditional sex therapy (the woman inserts the non-erect penis in her vaginal opening and tightens her muscles to hold it there). This is similar to second chakra connecting or *kareeza*, in which the man is inside the woman feeling their energy commingling but unconcerned with how erect he is, since energy can be transmitted regardless of the erection.

Traditional Sex Therapy versus Tanta

	Traditional Sex Therapy	Tantric Sex
Technique	Uses mind control, such as identifying grades of excitement and imagining steps on a ladder to measure excitement level.	Insists on awareness of energy and directing energy.
Recommended positions	Advises the man not to be on top, but rather the woman be on top, so he can relax.	The man can be on top to move energy more freely; preferred position is *yab yum* with female in male's lap.
Communicating with the partner	He gives her feedback.	Their energetic connection helps her sense where he is in the sexual response cycle.
Measuring success rates	Squeeze or stop-start training is 90 percent effective within 10 weeks	Considers measurement contrary to the experience of energy.

Tantric Meditation 5

Shaking in Sexual Embrace

This meditation also comes from the ancient text on Awareness called *Vigyan Bhairva* Tantra.

Shiva, the giver of the knowledge of Tantra and yoga, instructs his consort Devi: 'When in such embrace your senses are shaken as leaves, enter this shaking.'

This method can be a little difficult at first for modern lovers because we have learned to be so controlled in our sexuality. Condemnation by religion and society has created deep layers of guilt and shame so that even though we struggle to be free of these fetters it is not easy to be completely relaxed. Even those who have freed themselves from inhibitions may be relying on sexual technique, which is also a form of control, whereas this method requires a state of letting go.

Join your partner in your temple, creating a sensual atmosphere with music, lighting and incense. It is important that you have plenty of time and will not be disturbed.

* When you both feel ready, enter into the preliminaries of lovemaking, allowing your sexual energy to become aroused. You can be entwined in a deep sexual embrace, or simply embracing without generation. Bring your energy towards a peak but stay relaxed, not focused on a goal. A playful attitude helps, because this will encourage relaxation.
* In this state of sexual arousal and relaxation, tune into your bodies. Feel what they want to do, allow them to move, twist,

wrap themselves around each other, dance together, and shake together.

* It may be helpful to imagine that a wind is blowing and you are both trees, shaking in the wind. In fact, sex is a great wind. It is a very powerful energy, stirring all the cells in the body, igniting two bio-electrical circuits and flooding them with energy.

* Be spontaneous. Rather than focusing your attention on the sex centre, let sexual feelings spread all over your body. If your legs feel like shaking, let them shake.

* Don't allow your mind to keep you separate from the experience like an observer. Melt as deeply as possible into the sensations of your body. It is okay to take breaks, to be still for a while, and then follow a new impulse. After a while, you will feel that the level of passion and intensity remains by itself — there is no need to keep creating it. Your whole body will soon feel more sensual, more alive. It will begin to vibrate. Listen to these vibrations, cooperate with them, feel any subtle sensations and melt and merge with them.

* It is not physical sensations that are important, although at first they will be the main focus. Shiva talks about 'senses', so you can include taste, smell, sounds and vision. Let all your senses become involved in making love. Become drunk with your senses and enter more and more deeply into this drunkenness.

* Be sensitive to your partner, but stay tuned to your own sensations. This is a state of deep communion and yet you are focusing mainly on your own body. Paradoxically, through focusing on your own sensations, you will begin to experience that there are not two bodies involved, but only one organism. You begin to melt and merge with each other. This is a state of Tantric communion where duality is lost and oneness is found.

6

Taste

'The ego always attaches itself to whatever will strengthen its illusionary senses of self.'

Advice from a Tantric Master

Most people tend to unconsciously carry a belief that the erogenous zones of the human body are limited simply to the genitals and other overtly sexual areas. The Tantrics have long known that the truth in fact is that the entire human body is a sexual zone, with each inch being covered by skin that is super sensitive to touch of different degrees and thus open to receiving pleasure.

To explore whole-body sex, you have to expand your vision of the sexual possibilities of the human body and its sensory abilities. Here are the ten most sensitive, sexual hot zones on the human body, along with a brief description of what works best to arouse your partner.

Face. Particularly the eyes, lips and ears, which respond well to licks, kisses and hot breath.

Scalp. Massage or stimulate this area by running your fingers through her/his hair.

Neck and shoulders. These are amongst the most sensitive of zones of the human body. Kiss, lick or caress the neck. Gently rub and massage the shoulders.

Chest and breasts. A centre of sexual pleasure. Stroke, massage and kiss. The breasts also can be lightly squeezed or kneaded.

Nipples. Extremely sensitive in both men and women. Stick with gentle lip and tongue touches; also try blowing on them or fondling them with your fingers.

Abdomen. Very responsive to light stroking and soft kisses.

Waist. Often an unexplored zone that can yield unexpected pleasurable results. Use firmer strokes, like holding and molding her/him in your hands.

Thighs. Particularly the inside of the thigh is extremely sensitive. Use light caresses and counterclockwise circular rubbing.

Back of the legs. The fleshy hamstrings are very sensitive. As is the area behind the knee. Use light combing strokes with your fingertips and gentle caresses.

Buttocks. Use more forceful, deeper touches on the butt cheeks, and sprinkle in some kisses, kneading or light spanking.

God Spot — The G-spot: The Hottest Hot Spot

The G-spot has taken on almost mythic proportions in the annals of sex. Proponents say it is the most powerful and mysterious of erogenous zones. And supposedly the hardest to find. Some medical experts say it's hard to find because it simply doesn't exist. They say that while there is no question some women have a region in the anterior wall of the vagina that is sensitive to touch, there is no conclusive scientific evidence that there is an anatomically distinct entity.

The Tantra Masters of ancient India have continuously talked about a special God Spot inside the yoni of a woman which when located and stimulated will bring pleasure unlike any that she has experienced before. In fact, they termed it the God spot because it brings pleasure so intense, it literally transports you to the bliss of God in the moment. Women were encouraged to locate their own God spot and stimulate it to keep their body, mind and being in harmony and bliss.

While scientists and doctors in the Western world may continue to debate its existence, here's what we know. Named after Ernst Grafenberg, a German obstetrician/gynaecologist who discovered it in the 1940s while researching birth control, the G-spot is defined as a conglomeration of nerve endings, blood vessels and glands amassed around a woman's urethra on the inside, front wall of her vagina. Even proponents concede it apparently does not exist in all women. And when it does, they say, it's indistinguishable from surrounding tissue until she becomes deeply aroused. Then it swells and protrudes, until it feels like a firm, fleshy knob.

Some experts say the G-spot acts as a magic sex button for some women and is responsible for female ejaculation, a phenomenon not unlike that of a man, except that a woman ejaculates clear fluid, not sperm.

If you and your partner are curious about the G-spot, by all means, check it out. But keep in mind this important word of caution from Dr Goodstone: 'Remember that there hasn't been enough research to say whether the G-spot exists for all women. So if a woman can't find her G-spot, it doesn't mean there's anything wrong with her. Maybe she's not relaxed enough. Maybe it doesn't exist in some people. Maybe it atrophies if it hasn't been touched. We just don't know enough to say.'

Here are two ways for men to attempt to locate and stimulate the God-spot in your lover.

Get on your knees. Ask your partner to lie down on a bed with some pillows under her hips, so that her legs are spread and her bottom is slightly raised. Straddle her torso, facing her feet, so that you're supporting most of your body weight on your knees. With a slow, gentle touch, stimulate your partner's clitoris. When she's really aroused, slip two fingers into her vagina, keeping your hand palm up so that your fingertips can brush against the front, top part of her vaginal wall. If she has the G-spot you'll feel a small knob of firm flesh about the size of a bean or two. As you stimulate her G-spot, don't be surprised if she explodes with ecstasy and gushes fluid. Many women say orgasms stimulated from the G-spot are more intense than clitoral orgasm.

Position yourself for success. Another way to stimulate the G-spot is to use proper positioning. Certain sex positions allow better G-spot stimulation than others. Your best bets are most woman-on-top positions and nearly all rear-entry ones. These allow your penis to contact the vaginal wall head-on, so to speak, thus stimulating her G-spot better.

The God-spot is the gateway to sexual heaven for your partner; so to become a conscious and enlightened lover, locate it and bring her to her bliss by loving it.

Remember another thing; most men enjoy having their genitals touched at any time, whether they are sexually aroused or not. This is not usually the case with women. One of the most common complaints from women is that men immediately hone in on breasts and genitals.

Think of the vagina as a potential opening, a magical door that will happily open wide to receive you, but only after you have called ahead to ensure your welcome. Be certain she's eager for your genital explorations by focusing loving attention on other parts of her body first — lots of kissing, neck nuzzling, tender strokes on back, shoulders, and arms, then adoring caresses of her breasts.

Tantra says that you must build her arousal from the outside in. That is, start with her head, neck, hands, feet, then move in toward breasts, belly, and vagina. Only after you sense she's ready, through signs like rapid breathing, flushed skin, hardened nipples, or enticing moans should you move to her vagina. Once your hand or mouth is at her fountain of nectar, begin to explore it also from the outside inward — outer lips, clitoris, inner lips, vaginal canal.

Pay particular attention to her clitoris, her 'pleasure pearl' as the Taoist texts call it. The skin of your fingers is not nearly as sensitive as her clitoral tissue. But the tissue of your mouth and tongue is an almost perfect match. Begin with oral stimulation then move on to manual pleasuring. For some women the head of the clitoris, the pointed tip, is too sensitive for much direct pressure, so focus your attention on the sides. Touch around it and along the shaft until her excitement increases. Start slow and soft, then experiment with different pressures, strokes, and speeds. Ask her which ones she likes best. A good way to do this is to try two different touches, then ask her which one she likes better.

Remember, a master of Tantra is a master at the art of using his tongue! Though he uses the whole body as a sexual organ, he is aware that the tongue offers strengths that no other part of his body can. It is also through the tongue that he can give the greatest pleasure to his partner, not through his hands or his lingam as is wrongly believed.

If she's willing, invite her to masturbate for you so you can learn exactly how she likes to be touched. Many women are shy to do this at first but with some gentle encouragement she may really show her wanton self. It can be a great turn-on for both of you.

Once you do begin to explore her yoni, continue the movement of outside to inside — gently stimulating the outer lips, and especially the clitoris before you dip into the well of life. It is a good idea to wait until she is very aroused before entering her yoni either with your fingers or your penis. It should be wet and juicy before you go exploring. Generally, if she's not wet, she's not ready. It is as simple as that. If your lover does not have a lot of natural vaginal juices, even when she is fully aroused, be sure to use a good silicone or water-based lubricant. Nothing can be a quicker turn-off than rough, dry skin rubbing on soft vaginal tissues. Water-based or silicone lubricant is better because oil can clog the sensitive vaginal tissue. A delightful turn-on is to ask your woman, reverently and hotly, if you may enter. If she says she would like you to play a little more on the outside, do so with grace and love.

A wonderful way to make the transition from the outside of the yoni to the inside is to keep pleasuring her clitoris with your tongue as you slip a finger inside. Begin to stimulate her G-spot. Move your index finger or your first two fingers in a 'come hither' motion (as if you were asking someone from across the room to come over to where you are) and gently stroke her.

Tantra knows that women respond strongly to multiple points of stimulation — for instance, your tongue on her clitoris, your index finger in her yoni, your baby finger lightly circling her anus, and your other hand caressing her breasts.

Another key to pleasing a woman is this: When you find a stroke or movement that feels good to her, (for instance a long, slow rhythmic sliding on the shaft of her clitoris, or a short, rapid, medium-pressure stroke on her G-spot) keep on doing it! A common tendency is to want to add more — more speed, more pressure — or to move to some other spot. Instead, stay where you are and keep doing exactly what you are doing until she indicates that she would like something else, either by words or body movement.

Sometimes after a woman has had a clitoral orgasm, her clitoris feels too sensitive for continued caresses, particularly of the same intensity. Rather than moving on to some other delightful activity, you can help her to build to multiple clitoral orgasms with this simple technique:

* Maintain very light contact between tongue and clitoris, keeping absolutely still.
* After a short period of time, 10 to 30 seconds, move your tongue ever so slightly.
* If her response lets you know it is too much too soon, stop but keep the connection.
* After another brief pause, move your tongue again.
* Keep doing this until her body has calmed enough for you to resume active caressing, taking her up to yet another climax.

Tantra advises that it is also important that you let your lover know that you are enjoying pleasing her.

Remember, many women begin to worry that they are taking too long for their partner, that he is losing interest. This takes focus away from the pleasurable sensations in her body and jumps your lover into her head, just the opposite effect from what you would like — a letting go into the delights of your touch. So let her know by sounds, by words, that you love giving her this pleasure.

An intercourse technique that is highly pleasurable for women is the 'shallow-deep thrust'. This powerful thrusting method mixes a series of shallow thrusts — usually nine, an auspicious masculine number in Eastern philosophy — with one deep. Air is pushed out of the yoni by one deep plunge. The following shallow thrusts, which penetrate only the first inch and a half to two inches of the vaginal canal, create a vacuum that aches to be filled by the next deep one. These short strokes also stimulate the nerve-filled, most sensitive part of the yoni, increasing the woman's desire.

Besides giving her great pleasure, this technique helps you last longer because shallow thrusts do not build your excitement as quickly.

Each woman has her own path to orgasm. Many women reach orgasm through stimulation of the clitoris, others through internal vaginal stimulation and other through a simultaneous combination of internal and external pleasuring. Some tip over into climax with breast play, others by squeezing or applying pressure genitally, others through the power of erotic thought. The important thing is to relax into the delight of finding what your unique pleasure pattern is, not to make it essential to have a particular type of orgasm.

Generally, women reach climax most easily through clitoral stimulation, even during intercourse. Because the clitoris is extremely sensitive to touch of all kinds, experiment with caressing all the parts of it in different ways with a variety of things — tongue, fingers, feathers, and so on.

The most sensitive part of a woman's vaginal canal is the first inch to two inches. It is here that most of the nerve endings are located. As I explained earlier, the G-spot (God spot, or even sometimes called The Goddess spot) is the 'female prostate gland'. It surrounds the urethra (the same way a man's prostate surrounds his urethra) and is felt through the upper or top vaginal wall about half way between the back of the pubic bone and the cervix.

With proper stimulation and high states of sexual arousal, the G-spot can become very sensitive and may be a source of great pleasure. Stimulation of the goddess-spot can produce extraordinarily intense orgasms. If you are a woman being loved, as you are approaching a G-spot orgasm, you may feel like you have to urinate (probably because of the pressure against the urethra as the female prostate surrounding it swells). This may provoke you to tighten up, stop, and pull back from the edge of bliss. If, instead, you can stay relaxed or even push out a little with your vaginal muscles, that uncertain sensation will pass and you will likely move on into deep waves of sexual delight.

You may also have an ejaculatory orgasm. The Tantrics say that a fluid that resembles watered down fat-free milk — often lots of it — may spurt out from the urethra. It may have a slightly sweet taste. According to contemporary medical research, the female ejaculatory fluid contains simple sugars, glucose and fructose, as well as other ingredients. When it dries, it leaves no mark. This fluid is assumed to originate in the para-urethral glands, in the spongy tissue around the urethra.

As you become more and more open and charged up through extended lovemaking your entire yoni may come alive with sensation so that you experience orgasm deep within the vaginal canal. Continued PC squeezing magnifies the intensity of the orgasm.

Women do not usually notice a loss of sexual energy after orgasm. In fact, one orgasm can be the building block for the next and the next. However if you do find your desire diminishing after a particular type of orgasm, delay it, building up to several peaks and backing off before you let go.

Mixing saliva and yoni juice is a Tantric favourite. This one is a special practice of the Tantric adepts. When you are having oral sex with a woman, the mouth fills with saliva. Mix this saliva with the yoni juice of your partner. Think of it forming a special elixir and drink deeply of it. Any repugnance to oral sex is often due to widespread confusion about the difference between bodily excretions, which are waste products no longer needed, and sexual secretions, which are fluids rich in nutrients.

Of course, good genital hygiene is a pre-requisite for this practice. If your woman has any form of discharge or any consistent type of vaginal infection, don't use this practice. Share these practices with your partner only if you feel she is ready. It is a wise lover who doesn't introduce his partner to things before she is ready. If it's going to frighten or to turn her off in any way, tell her about them a little bit at a time. In the meantime, you can practice them yourself.

Both Tantric and Taoist traditions had many advanced practices for absorption of the woman's essence. These practices were carried out in deep secrecy. In the ancient texts there are many stories of men and women, living well into their hundreds, who practised absorbing each other's essences. Normally in a healthy relationship any loss of female yin essence is compensated for with absorption of the male yang essence.

Ancient Indian and Chinese masters clearly understood the power of Shakti (the feminine energy), and had numerous concubines and ancient Hindu rituals in which the man would make love to many women on the one night before implanting his seed into his special number one wife. There are many stories of men living into their hundreds with at least 20 wives — and keeping them all satisfied. These stories were common in olden times.

Not only did the ancient masters believe that it would raise their consciousness and awareness, they also realized that it was the nectar, the elixir of everlasting life. Thus as they kept the secrets from the masses they appeared as gods, men of wisdom. This was one of the secrets of their charisma.

You don't need 20 wives to absorb the Shakti, because one beloved has all the Shakti you can possibly handle. Your woman's Shakti may be suppressed now, but believe me, the potential is unlimited. You need to work as teammates to awaken it. The secret is to realize that for your beloved to open up to that much Shakti, she really has to trust you.

Trust, love, commitment, and practice are all important. Together you go on this journey. Whenever resistances come up for either you or your beloved, instead of abandoning the relationship work through these problems to reach another level. And always enjoy the journey to opening more Shakti — it's unlimited.

Pleasuring the Man

And now a word for the Shaktis out there. Once you have decided to pleasure your partner, the manifestation of it is a fairly simple process. Tell your partner a few exciting promises about how the evening will go. Although men are sometimes not verbal, often responding to just action, Tantric lovemaking stimulates all the senses, which includes offering verbal statements about your love, what you want to do, and reassurances.

Men also often like to be in control, so giving your partner some clues about what is happening and what will happen, will probably make your partner feel more relaxed. Say just enough to put your partner at ease but not too much; that would be a distraction or engage his mind.

The Idea of Tantric Sex is to Feel the Body and to Quieten the Mind.

Use the following four R's as guidelines:

Reassure your Partner. Assure him that he does not have to perform or do anything to please you. 'You don't have to do anything to please me. I'm here totally to please you tonight.' 'This night is totally for you.' As the pleasuring progresses, add statements such as, 'You don't have to have an erection or get excited, just enjoy the feelings in your body.' By doing this you remove all responsibility of performance from your partner and release him from any expectations that he may feel you have. Such a feeling can be very freeing for a man and will make him connect with you in deep gratitude and love you even more.

Relax your Partner. Say, 'I'm going to massage you to relax you and you just have to lay there and enjoy the sensations.' 'You can tell me what to do that you would particularly like'. Once again, it's extremely pleasurable for your partner to feel he can tell you whatever he wishes you to do and that you will do it.

Relieve your Partner. Constantly tell him that you are enjoying what you are doing, so he does not worry. Even though men may enjoy what you are doing to them, they also tend to consequently worry whether you are enjoying what you are doing. Any self-aware man would want his partner's pleasure too, even as she continues to give him pleasure. So remove this thought from his mind by clearly stating that you are enjoying this as much as he is.

Reward your Partner. Men (just like women) love to be acknowledged, so tell your partner how delighted you are with him as a person. Compliment who he is and tell your partner what you particularly like about his being and his body. A sincere compliment is balm to the soul, and coming from a lover in the throes of deep passion goes to the depth of your being.

Breathing Techniques to assist your Loving

Prana has been said to translate as breath. In fact the Sanskrit word prana means 'life force' or 'life energy'.

It is this life force that is the creative power of the cosmos — it is believed by Tantrics that it is possible to live on prana, to use prana to overcome the limitations of the physical body, and transcend the limits of the material world.

There are several simple breathing techniques that can assist you in your lovemaking. Some I have described earlier in the book, here are some more from the yogic teachings for you to experiment with.

Bhramari Breath

* Exhale, contracting the abdominal muscles to expel it, and then inhale through the nose, while making a buzzing sound like a bee.
* Retain it for a few seconds, as long as comfortable, then exhale as before but this time making a humming sound — similar to the mantra Om.
* Work toward longer retentions — and concentrating on storing the prana energy in the solar plexus (*manipura* chakra, literally

manipura means 'jewel of great consciousness', or the 'jewel in the lotus') and visualize separating the prana from ordinary air.

* Focus on the sounds during inhalation and exhalation — and on the vital life energy being stored and saved during breath retention.
* Each in breath, retention, and out breath, counts as one cycle.
* Being with five or so cycles, and adding more as you become more adept.

Complete Breath

Most people breathe too shallowly, and even those who draw breath down to the abdomen may not be doing it correctly.

* Blow out all air, using the abdomen, chest, and throat, to expel it. Inhale deeply, pulling the breath into the abdomen. Continue inhaling filling the rib cage and lungs. Retain the air for a few seconds — keeping the body relaxed.
* Now exhale slowly, using the stomach, ribcage, and throat, to gradually force all air out. Work up to longer inhalation, retention, and exhalations. Do not count with a clock. Allow your body to be your clock. The ratio should be 1:1:1 with the Complete Breath, unlike certain other prana techniques.

The Complete Breath increases oxygen supply to the blood haemoglobin levels and promotes mental relaxation. It also slows the heart rate, and has a calming effect on central nervous system. The Complete Breath is commonly used with many Hatha Yoga exercises.

Vital Breath

This is very easy and it strengthens the lungs, and energizes the body.

* Breathe in through nose in short sharp sniffs until the lungs are expanded to capacity.
* Blow out through mouth, making a loud 'HAAA' sound.

* Focus on bringing in energizing prana, blowing out all tension, negativity, and anything you feel separates you from realizing your objectives.

Kapala-Bhati

This is also quite easy to master. There are many variations — this one is the simplest, but no less effective than more advanced practices.

* Sit with legs crossed; back and head kept straight. Inhale through the nose, mouth closed, and sneeze. With mouth closed the lower abdomen will balloon out. Snap it back in sharply. Begin with 10-15 rounds; work up to 50 and above — naturally without forcing.
* You should feel nothing in upper lungs, chest, or throat area.
* Fix your attention on solar plexus chakra.
* After completion, sit quietly, being aware of any bodily changes and mental effects.

On a purely physical level, *kapala-bhati* also pumps oxygen in, increases haemoglobin levels, has a soothing effect on many glands, and can be used for relief by asthmatics or smokers.

Prana-Vayu Rasa

This is a recharging breath cycle. It should be performed standing, eyes closed, the mind focused on *anja* chakra — the 'third eye' chakra, at the centre and just above the physical eyes.

* Inhale, swinging the arms twice backward and twice forward vigorously. Exhale.
* Inhale, stretching the arms forward at 90-degree angle from body, and then swing them out sideways at the shoulder level twice. Exhale, and drop the arms.
* Inhale, swing the arms up twice and down twice, parallel at sides, arching the small of the back slightly. Exhale, and drop the arms.

* Inhale and hold the breath while stretching the arms forward. Then clench the fists and pull them against the chest.
* Retain the breath while shaking entire body. Exhale.
* Inhale, swinging the arms overhead and bend the body to the right from the waist, but not allowing the ribcage to collapse. Focus on the parts being stretched. Exhale while straightening, and then repeat the exercise to the left.
* Inhale. Retain the breath, and massage the ribs. Exhale. Inhale. Retain the breath, patting the breasts or the pectoral muscles. Exhale.

The idea of this recharging prana is to tap into individual life force — Atman — and unite it with universal energy — Brahman. Physically, it energizes, provides limbering of the body, cleanses and exercises the lungs.

Prana Sukha — The Healing Breath

Literally, 'breath of joy' or 'joyous life force'. Change the time spent on each part of the breathing cycle.

The rhythm of Prana Sukha is said to be perfectly suited to extraction of vital energy from the atmosphere. The ratio of inhalation, retention, exhalation is 1:4:2.

In other words, inhale, hold breath four times as long as inhalation takes, then exhale, taking twice as long as inhalation. The inhalation establishes the time ratio for the other two — making sure it does not become uncomfortable. Generally, begin by inhaling just slightly longer than when breathing unconsciously, the same with retention and exhalation. Then gradually increase.

Sukha slows down the breathing process, which is beneficial to both body and mind.

Do not count either mentally or verbally — counting is a natural, and unconscious, temptation but interferes with the meditative process. Instead, measure the rhythm against pulse, heartbeat, or by focusing the mind on the sounds of inhalation and exhalation of breath —

this is the correct method, creating an audio rhythm and helps body and mind to merge.

The *Gheranda Samhita*, an ancient scripture on yoga, says: 'In entering, the breath makes the sound 'SO' and in exiting, the sound 'HAM'. Thus the breath makes the power word SOHAM — or, 'I am It'. The subtle sound reverberates in the root chakra, the heart chakra, and the third eye chakra. The Yogi should perform this repetition consciously.

Another measuring process is concentration on a mantra, such as '*aum*', or whatever is your personal preference.

Ways to Calm Yourself Down

Life is stressful, so understandably it might be difficult to do some of your Tantric practices if you aren't in the right frame of mind. Worrying about work, a health problem or a relationship can prevent you from directing your energy as you wish. If you are stressed, remember that enjoyment is moving away from you, and you will constantly be playing a catch-up game.

Here are some ways to calm down and relax your energy:

* Control your breath. Take a deep breath in to the count of seven and exhale to a longer count. Exhaling longer than you inhale relaxes you and decreases your heart rate.
* Sit still and empty your mind. Let thoughts come and go without focusing on them. Or try meditating on a single word, such as 'om' to calm your mind.
* Adjust your environment to eliminate distractions such as ringing phones, irritating street noise, or glaring bright lights.
* Light candles and soak in a warm bubble bath.
* Take a long walk, play with the dog, or toss a ball around with your kids. Just about any physical activity is a stress reducer.
* Close your eyes and picture a soothing scene, such as the ocean. Imagine the smell of the salt air and the feel of the sand between your toes.

* Soothe yourself with massage. Use long, smooth strokes to calm you while you breathe slowly and deeply. Use oil or cream to glide hour hands over your skin.

Some Facts about Tantra

* Tantric sex involves the union and balance of opposites, female and male energies referred to as yin and yang that symbolize dark and light, moon and sun, receiving and giving, heaven and earth.
* The Tantric *yab yum* position for lovemaking described in ancient Hindu texts in which the woman sits in the man's lap, helps align energies necessary for a powerful Tantric love connection.
* Tantric sex is not simply an act but the build-up, movement, and transmission of energy through your own body and between you and a partner.
* Setting boundaries by saying yes or no to what you want builds self-esteem and empowerment that is essential for a healthy interaction with a partner in Tantric sex.
* Honouring and respecting your partner is essential in Tantric sex. It is accomplished by asking permission for any sexual act and in using terms like 'beloved' to refer to your partner and 'sacred space', 'yoni', and 'lingam' to refer to sexual organs.
* Breathing practices are key to directing sexual energy to other parts of the body to connect with the beloved, maintain health, achieve ecstatic states, and melt into unity.
* There are seven energy centres called chakras throughout the body, each associated with colours, sounds, and issues. Tantric practices help you connect and use the energy in these centres to achieve desired feelings and connections in yourself and in a relationship.
* Practising breathing exercises with a partner can greatly intensify your love connection and achievement of mutual sexual satisfaction.

* Quieting the mind and directing energy is the key to reaching high states of consciousness in Tantric sex and can be accomplished through meditation on sounds and designs.
* Bliss is an ecstatic feeling of connection with a loving energy that expands inwardly and outwardly.
* Simple exercises can create intense pleasure and deep connection, for example, looking deeply into each other's eyes, sending energy through each other's hearts.
* Stimulate all your senses for a truly all-consuming Tantric experience; explore tastes, smells, sights, sounds and touches.
* Tantra believes that each one of us has particular thoughts, sounds or symbols that can trigger sensuous feelings; know what these 'love triggers' are for yourself and for your partner.
* Tantra believes that the most blissful sexual experiences can happen when you do not force any actions, but rather when you are still and allow the urges that come from within to move you.
* Instead of abruptly ending your lovemaking, stay in bliss by taking deliberate actions to stay connected.

Tantric Meditation 6

The Golden Light

This meditation is Taoist in origin and part of an ancient Chinese text called The Secret of the Golden Flower. Essentially, the method is Tantric in nature. It is a beautiful way to experience your body as a channel through which energy can flow freely and naturally.

It requires no preparation, because the best time to do it is in the early morning when you are just coming out of sleep, still drowsy and not yet fully awake — no need to take a shower first. You can do it without effort, just lying in bed, resting on your back. The meditation works with your breathing and your imagination.

With eyes closed, breathe in slowly. As you do so, imagine that a beautiful shower of golden light is entering through the top of your head and filling your whole body, all the way down to your feet, to the tips of your toes. By the time you have completed one in-breath, your whole body is filled with golden light.

As you breathe slowly out, imagine that a deep darkness is entering through your feet and filling your whole body, all the way to the top of your head. By the end of your out-breath, your whole body is filled with darkness.

Repeat this visualization with each breath: golden light flooding in through your head as you inhale, darkness flooding in through your feet as you exhale.

In Taoist terms, this creates a balance between your male energy, known as yang, and your female energy, called yin. The golden light is yang and the darkness is yin. The golden light is energizing and exhilarating; the darkness is soft, soothing and relaxing.

Do this for 20-30 minutes. If you find it difficult to do this meditation in the morning, you can also do it at night, when you are already in bed, as the last thing before you go to sleep.

7

Awareness

'There never was, and never will be, a time when your life is not now.'

Advice from a Tantric Master

Tantra is essentially the way to arrive at three states of being. The practice of Tantra leads us to the qualities of Love (Divinity), Light (knowledge) and Freedom (Bliss).

By our very existence, all of us have the ability to live every moment of our life in four different freedoms offered to us by the Universal Consciousness. So even as we go through the grind of our daily life we carry infinite freedom within us whether we realize it or not. Let us now look at the freedoms that we have access to.

The First Freedom: Body

Awaken your senses. See, hear, smell, taste, and feel love.

Know your body as a divine temple of love, carrier of the soul, manifestation of god and goddess. Become truly at home in your body — at ease, at peace, comfortable in your skin. Allow yourself to experience physical pleasure. Feed yourself and all around you with sublime, intimate human touch.

You are your body. Your body is freedom.

The Second Freedom Mind

There are no limits. All limits are self-imposed. Change thought from being your master to being your powerful servant, a tool of your liberation. Turn your thinking on, and turn it off, when you want to. You have the power over what you think. You also have the power over how you think about things. By how and what you think about, you create your life. Thoughts become things. The world gives us not what we desire but what we are. Connect with your higher self for guidance and direction.

You are your mind. Your mind is freedom.

The Third Freedom: Heart

Heal your broken heart. Open your healed heart. Give and receive love easily, naturally, spontaneously, and unconditionally. Discover your lover within. Love yourself. Accept yourself. Forgive yourself. **Know that you are worthy of love**. Acknowledge and welcome the love of others. Dare to be the great lover you are. Learn to listen to your inner voice that speaks to you from your heart. Know that your heart will bring you to fulfilment. Know that only in your heart will you become total and connect with another. Lead from your heart.

You are your heart. Your heart is freedom.

The Fourth Freedom: Soul

Your body, mind, and heart are windows to your soul. Your soul transcends space and time. It is outside of cause and effect. **Your soul is complete and perfect.** When you communicate with your higher self, with god and goddess, you are communicating with your soul. Your soul has your body, mind, and heart within it. Your soul is what you are. Your soul is what you arrive at when you break through all conditioning imposed upon you. Your soul is never bound nor can it be.

Your soul is The Soul. Your soul is freedom.

Tantra helps you explore these four freedoms and make them your reality, not just in your relationship, but in all areas of your life. Tantric practice works on four levels, corresponding to our four freedoms: body/physical, mind/mental, heart/emotional, and soul/energetic.

On the physical level, you learn very specific techniques for joyous and extended lovemaking.

On the mental level, you learn to shift habitual attitudes to sex, overcoming negative conditioning that may have taught you that sex is bad or shameful. Part of the Tantric training is developing the ability to focus, to become totally absorbed during lovemaking.

On the emotional level, you learn to trust, to let go and surrender, and to open your heart.

On the soul level, you go beyond previously perceived boundaries of who you think you are to connect in ways that are much more than physical. You think and believe your partner to be divine.

Tantra is about openness and transformation. Like most spiritual paths, sacred sex teaches a discipline of the mind and body. It does so amid joy and letting go of the sensual aspects of living. As a celebration of life, sacred sex teaches the importance of conscious awareness, of living totally within your actions. By focusing attention on your body and your mind, you become all-around healthier:

Your emotions become more stable and more real.

Your mental capacity increases.

Your physical health improves as you learn to honour your body as the temple of your soul.

As for your sexual life, the glories that await you when you begin to practice Tantra are beyond your imagination. The exercises and techniques fortify your entire uro-genital system; you gain muscle strength, improved circulation, and heightened sensitivity. You shift your approach to lovemaking and learn exquisite new ways to please your partner and yourself.

Ordinary lovemaking has a goal: orgasm. If you both orgasm at the same time, you have really hit the jackpot. If neither of you orgasm at all, you may as well have spent your time elsewhere.

In Tantric loving, there is no goal. There is a purpose, however, and that purpose is union. Every aspect of your Tantric loving serves that purpose. Your intention is to merge with your lover in all aspects — body, mind, heart, and soul — not just body. As you let go of the goal of orgasms, you actually begin to have more of them. Tantra is a sure-fire way to keep the purely physical experience of sex exciting, new, and fresh for even the most long-term lovers.

Many people experience occasional, spontaneous moments of blissful oneness with their partner, with nature, with the Divine, during peak sexual experiences. With practice, you can learn to consciously create this rapturous spiritual union.

As you master moving the sexual energy between your two bodies, you experience altered states of consciousness leading to ecstasy. In order to create enough sexual energy to move them into euphoric states of Divine connection, practitioners of Tantra make love for long periods of time, experiencing extraordinary levels of pleasure along the way.

Tantric lovemaking involves conscious breathing, muscle contraction exercises, sound, visualization, meditation, sensual massage, sexual play, creating a sacred loving space, and other rituals. Largely through ceremony and ritual, we access our deepest consciousness and the soul. This aspect of Tantra, perhaps more than any other, transforms ordinary friction sex into energy sex and ultimately, if love is truly present, into what we call soul sex.

As a great master once expressed it, 'When love and skill work together, expect a masterpiece'.

For example, in traditional Tantric practice, lovers begin to see themselves as the god and goddess Shiva and Shakti. They leave their daily selves behind and become manifestations of the gods. If Shiva and Shakti do not have a personal meaning for you, but if your spiritual perception is that god or goddess or Creator is within you, you can employ a similar mental picture to let that divinity out. You can focus on expanding that essence of the Divine within so that it encompasses you entirely — you and your lover become All. Speak aloud your intention as you join in passion together: 'We are divine, we are one, we are All in our love.' Show appreciation for the connection you share: 'Thank you for this bliss'.

Perhaps you do not have a particular faith, or you may not consider yourself a spiritual person. Often, people who do not see themselves as being particularly spiritual, but who practice Tantra for an improved sex life and more intimate relationship, find that with Tantric loving a spiritual awakening happens spontaneously.

The practices of breathing, being in the moment, mindfulness, opening your heart, surrender and letting go, moving sexual energy, and the experiences these practices bring (altered states of consciousness), lead to a connection that is more than physical. It leads out from the self in union and transcendence, to the partner, to the Divine, so a spiritual sensibility is awakened. You become simultaneously, a highly sexual and a spiritual person.

The 7 Essential Wisdom Secrets of Tantra

And now we arrive at the most important part of this book — the essential wisdom secrets you need to become a true Tantric adept of love and of life. You have probably been picking up on them throughout the sharing, but here they are for you all laid out in perfect order. It is important to remember that they are attitudes that you carry both into your loving and also into your living, everyday of your life.

Remember, more than all the Tantric techniques and meditations in this book so far, Tantra is essentially about a way to live every moment of your life. Tantra is an attitude. An attitude that you bring to everything you do, and not only to your lovemaking. Tantra is about all moments of life, not just the intimate one with your partner.

Tantra is not what you do, but what you become.

Practice these secrets, make them a part of your being, incorporate them in what you do, and transform your life from base metal into gold. Become an alchemist, of your own life force. As I often like to say, all life is Tantra!

Understanding the teachings and the inherent attitude of Tantra will greatly increase your ability to experience spiritual sexual ecstasy. Here are the seven essential secrets that all Tantric lovers know and practice in their experience of loving, each other, the life force itself and all of existence around them.

Secret 1 — Learn to Love your Self by Loving Another

Love begins at home, with loving yourself.

This doesn't mean self-centred indulgence, but the ability to trust yourself and to listen to your inner voice — the intuitive guidance of your own heart.

The Tantric adept know that true fulfilment will only come from listening to the voice of the heart and having the courage to follow it. Loving yourself means that you realize that you deserve the experience of ecstasy; loving yourself also means that you are not willing to compromise or settle for less than you really want, especially in sex.

Trying to love another when you do not love yourself does not work. You end up feeling possessive, jealous, and dependent. By contrast, when you really begin to love yourself, you become a magnet, attracting the love of others.

Yet you don't need the others to feel whole. Love then is not a desperate need to fill something up within yourself, it becomes a state of being. Out of your own sense of abundance, you want to share and celebrate — you are grateful to receive and to give.

This is freedom, the basis of true partnership. This is the goal of spiritual sex.

In Tantric sex you honour each other's differences, yet you move beyond them into a space of respect and devotion.

Ways to Love Yourself by Loving Another

Discover the Body with Love. Take a loving visual, tactile tour of your mate's body. Create a sensual ambience for your body discovery. Make sure the room is warm. Lighting should be bright enough to see clearly but soft and caressing to your skin, for example candles or a red light bulb. Play music that relaxes you and makes you feel sensual.

Begin by asking your lover's permission: 'My beloved (or your name for your lover), I come to you with love, desire, and the utmost respect. May I please explore your wonderful body?' Your lover responds: 'Yes, I welcome you with love and trust.' You can make up your own words to show respect, love, trust, and care. Sometimes, the receiving partner may be shy or uncomfortable having a particular body segment thoroughly explored. If this is the case, it is important to be open and honest. Tell each other how you feel, and respect your limitations.

Begin from a distance with a slow, soft caressing look from head to toe and back again. As you are looking, tell your lover what pleases you about her. Remember most of us are not accustomed to being gazed at all over, especially with love and adoration and desire. Your partner may be feeling uncomfortable — ask her to breathe deeply, to relax any tension in her body, and to try to feel the vital energy coming from your eyes into her body.

Move closer and mix your looking with touches. Go slowly. Begin with her hands, lifting them, caressing her palm, stroking it lightly then gently sucking each finger. Work your way up her arms, feathering lightly with your fingers, repeating the path with a sniffing, tickling nose, repeat again with pouting, nibbling lips and darting, slippery tongue. As you explore, keep letting your lover know how much you are enjoying your tour — tell her with words, sounds, facial gestures. Look into each other's eyes frequently and feel the connection between the two of you deepening.

From arms, move up to her head, neck, ears, then eyes, face, mouth, chin, and back down to her neck. Take your time. Feel her skin beneath your hands, smell the unique scent of each part of her, listen to her breath and to any sounds she may make in response to your touch. Switch from her head to her feet. Play with them as you did with her hands. Then proceed up her legs. Take your time. Be playful. Focus all your attention on your lover and allow your heart to open.

When you reach the tops of her legs, roll her on to her stomach and explore her back with your hands, then your nose, then your mouth, and combinations of all three, from the base of her neck all the way down to her feet.

Once again, roll her on to her back and starting at the hollow of her neck work your way down her torso in waves using your hands, nose, and mouth. Pause at breasts and belly or other spots on her torso that give both of you pleasure. Finally, turn your attention to her yoni (vagina). This is the seat of creation, the wellspring of life. Explore her gently with nose, mouth, and fingers.

Your purpose is to heighten awareness for both of you, not to turn her on (although this may happen). Do not use habitual touches that you know will bring her to orgasm. If either, or both, of you become sexually excited, relax and be with the excitement. This is an opportunity to feel the body electric — to raise and keep the energy high without going over the edge to release. If your charge is too intense, try deep, slow breathing and grounding. You may be surprised to find that the loving body discovery can also be more relaxing and affectionate than sexually stimulating. Whatever happens is right.

Finish with a complete hug — head to toe for two minutes. Feel your hearts beating. Match your breathing rhythm. In love and respect, thank each other, and then switch partners.

Remember, the Body Discovery is not a massage, nor is it done with the intention of arousing your lover sexually, nor is it leading up to intercourse or an orgasmic climax. Separate the Body Discovery from these other ways of being intimate so you can experience being in the moment without trying to get somewhere in your lovemaking.

You can discover the joy of touching each and every part of your lover's body, and learn that every touch is potentially as satisfying and wonderful as any other. This is also an excellent exercise in which to move beyond the anxiety of responsibility to 'perform' sexually, to make it happen for your partner.

Conscious Breathing. One of the essential tools of Tantric loving, conscious breathing not only brings you into the moment so you can participate fully in an intimate sexual exchange, it also fortifies your reproductive system and heightens your sexual pleasure. In addition, your overall health benefits when you breathe properly — aches and pains, tension and anxiety disappear; your body cells charge up with more oxygen and your brain energizes for clear thinking.

Breath control during lovemaking opens you up for extended pleasure and multiple orgasms. When you want more arousal and excitement, breathe rapidly (panting); when you want to sustain riding the edge of sexual pleasure, breathe slowly and deeply.

Conscious breathing helps you learn to surrender and to ask for what you want. Focusing on a long, slow exhalation (twice as long as your inhalation) assists you to let go. Extending your inhalation for twice as long as your exhalation aids in developing your assertiveness and self-confidence so you can express your desires.

Breathing in harmony with your partner is a powerful way to cultivate your sexual relationship and strengthen your energetic connection.

Deep Belly Breathing. This exercise helps you learn to breathe deeply and consciously:

* Sit, or lie down in a quiet, comfortable place.
* Loosen up by contracting and then releasing all the parts of your body.
* Start at your feet — tighten, hold, let go.
* Move to your calves — tighten, hold, let go.
* And so on, all the way up to your head.
* Remember the muscles in your face, neck, and scalp — you may be surprised at how much tension they hold.
* When your body is relaxed, begin to focus on your breathing. Place your right hand on your abdomen and your left hand along the bottom of your ribs on your left side.
* Inhale through your nose, slowly, deeply, naturally. Feel the air coming in through your nostrils. Follow it all the way down to your belly.

* Your belly should rise as you begin your inhale; you may even push it out a little to help your re-learn to breathe very deeply.
* Continue to fill your lungs by expanding your rib cage.
* Feel your ribs moving outward as you inhale. You may even push them out a little to help you.
* Continue inhaling, filling the upper portion of your lungs.
* Inhale until your lungs and even your throat, mouth, and nose are completely full of air.
* Use a slow count of five to time your inhalation.
* As soon as you are full of air, begin to exhale.
* Do not hold your breath or stop between inhaling and exhaling.
* Allow a smooth transition from 'in' to 'out'.
* Exhale slowly through your nose, counting to nine.
* Pay attention to the sensation of air as it passes.
* Inhale again and follow the breath down into your belly bringing with it vital energy.
* Exhale and imagine all negativity, illness, or tension leaving your body.
* Continue to inhale and exhale slowly.
* If thoughts intrude, gently call your attention back to your breath.
* Follow each breath, slow and deep.
* Do this exercise for a minimum of 10 minutes.

If you fall asleep while you are practising, have a nice nap!

Harmonizing Your Breathing. During Tantric lovemaking, partners often consciously, and sometimes even unconsciously, harmonize their breathing. You can do this for different effects.

At the outset of your loving time, sitting quietly together, looking into each other's eyes and breathing in synchronicity will help you tune in to each other and tune out the rest of the world. Breathing slowly and deeply in this fashion will also relax you and help you focus on the present moment.

When you are both highly aroused and want to move the energy you have built up with your love play, stop active lovemaking. For instance, if you are engaged in intercourse, stay joined but stop thrusting. Become still, look into each other's eyes, and breathe slowly and deeply together focusing on moving your high sexual energy up from your genitals throughout your body. This will also deepen your emotional and energetic connection and help you prolong your pleasure.

Experiment with these variations of breathing rhythm: Both partners inhale and exhale at the same time. One partner inhales while the other exhales.

Counting Breaths. Counting breaths is a familiar exercise for students of Meditation and Zen. This is an excellent practice to help you learn to stay focused on the now moment.

Begin to count your breaths up to 10. Then start over at one and count to 10 again. Repeat this for the period of time you have chosen for your practice. Keep your mind only on your counting of breaths. When other thoughts intrude, do not try to get rid of them, just bring your attention back to your counting. Try to work up to where you can do 300 counts (10 counted 30 times). This must be done without distracting thoughts of any kind before you can claim to have done it. Depending upon how slowly you breathe, counting to 300 will take close to three hours! A good start is to get as far as 30 counts (10 counted three times) without distracting thoughts.

Secret 2 — Stop Feeling Guilty

Tantric sex teaches you to drop your guilt about sex. You may think you have already done this, but guilt goes very deep, below our conscious thoughts. Why? Because for centuries organized religions have used guilt about sex as a subtle way of manipulating and exploiting people, and the recent liberalization of sexuality has not yet succeeded in erasing this cruel legacy.

Remember that all guilt arises from thoughts that are anchored in the past and that includes your conditioning which began since the time you were born. Being in the present moment totally, it is impossible to carry guilt, since you are completely absorbed in the moment itself and the trigger for feeling guilt is missing.

As soon as guilt is felt, your being is divided between the past and the 'now', and you will never experience totality in this moment of loving. You must learn to experience sex as a healthy drive — a celebration of life that keeps you youthful and alive. You must strive to become total in every moment of your loving without any conditioning of the past or any worry about the future.

Ways to Stop Feeling Guilty

Immerse Yourself in Experience. Immersion is something you do, not something that happens to you.

Realizing this is a key to opening yourself to experience immersion, which in turn is essential for experiencing ecstasy. Until you understand this, you may be tempted to give credit for the peak experiences you have to the circumstances of the experience or to the other person(s) involved, if there were any. Once you know that immersion is something you do, you can learn exactly how you do it and you can do it more often. With mastery, you can immerse yourself any time, in any experience you want to.

Drop the Past, Detach from the Future. Learn to simply drop the past and all voices associated with it. Detach from all worry and anxiety of the future, including of the next moment to follow. Make no judgements of this present moment based on any conditioning or experiences of the past. Become total now, in this moment. Be fully present here and available to the lover before you.

When you try to do this you realize that it's almost impossible ... unless, you come into this moment totally free and with an attitude of pure and total open-ness to what it brings. In this state of mind, judgements cannot exist. Guilt vanishes and you become free in total surrender and acceptance of what the potential of this moment holds for you.

Secret 3 — Enjoy Spontaneity

We have a tendency to trust experts, methods, and techniques while denying our own spontaneous feelings. You may be a victim of this attitude, which relies too much on external guidance and inhibits your ability to follow sudden changes in the way your energy is flowing.

In Tantric sex you accept the idea that life is a great mystery. In addition to learning techniques, you give yourself the freedom to respond to the new and unfamiliar in the way that feels natural.

Ways to Enjoy Spontaneity

Break the Bondage of Memory. Memory can rob you of being in the moment. Memory is quick to fill in the blanks, completing your thought, or your sensory impression, before the whole has been received and integrated into your experience. You remember the last time you saw something and you see it as you remember it, rather than as it is now. You do the same with all the senses — smelling what you have always smelled, hearing what you have heard before. You do not walk up the stairs now, you walk up the same stairs you have walked up countless times, without any awareness of what you are doing. You touch your lover's body from memory. It is not real skin; it is the skin you remember having touched hundreds of times before.

Running on memory is like running on empty. There is just not enough juice in memory to sustain excitement, motivation, and passion. You want something new; you want variety. If you touch new skin, if you see a different body, you pay attention in a way that makes you aware that you are alive. After all, as the saying goes, 'Variety is the spice of life.' But you do not need to find variety and newness outside. Variety does not just come from what you see, but rather how you see it. If you really pay attention, you can train yourself to take in information through your senses as if for the very first time. Once you learn to consciously stay in the moment, then no matter how many times you have touched, tasted, smelled, or seen your lover's skin, it will be unique and new each and every time.

Drop Expectations. All expectations are like making an appointment with the future. The future is a moment that has not yet been created, nor crystallized. Its potential and its outcome is totally unknown, thus having expectations about what's going to happen or what should happen, is putting a chain on a moment that's inherently free.

My master often used to say that having expectations is like making an appointment with the future moment. Then he would coyly add, 'And where there is appointment, disappointment is sure to follow.'

The message is clear: expectations bind you and take away the freedom that spontaneity offers. Drop your expectations and be free and happy.

Secret 4 — Have a 'Beginner's Mind'

The practice of Zen and meditation both strive to develop what the masters call a 'Beginner's mind'. This is a state that is constantly open to the possibilities of the moment, every moment, without any roots in the past and any expectations of the future.

The Tantric adept believes that existing in this state of awareness lays the potential of the moment at you feet, you begin to operate from the most natural and connected state of being without letting the past and the future intrude upon your present moment, which is seen as a gift of existence to you.

The Awakened Masters of all the different religions believed that *every moment offers you infinite potential for awakening* regardless of the activity that's being performed in the moment, as long as your state of awareness can become total in it.

The same awareness is to be carried into your lovemaking, which then makes every experience and every touch like for the first time.

The mind and the body are completely free to simply be, and to experience, without the chains of the past experiences or the future expectations binding or weighing you down.

The moment before you now is your only reality and to be total in it is the only attempt of the enlightened lover.

Ways to Develop a Beginner's Mind

Be Here Now. Although you will make love thousands of times in your years together, your lovemaking will be fresh and immediate, if each time you make love, you are fully in the moment. With 100 percent of your senses zeroed in on exactly what is going on at the moment, you will be able to see and feel everything anew.

By learning to be here now, you can have a dynamic and vital connection with your lover, not just during sex, but also in all your activities, and you can extend that zest over a lifetime together. It's likely that you have already experienced being wholly in the moment, for example, when you were enraptured by music, or the setting sun or immersed in dancing, running, creating, or lovemaking. In such moments, time and space seem to disappear. Your senses are hyper-alert. Your heart is at peace. All is right and complete.

Although you would like more of these experiences, you may believe that you have little or nothing to do with creating them, that they are occurrences completely outside your realm of influence. Yet being here now is a state of consciousness. It is only marginally related to the circumstances of a situation, and in no way dependent on them, You can learn to be in the now moment at any time or place, under any set of circumstances, positive or negative.

Being in the moment — totally immersed in your actions — is a simple concept; one you would think should also be simple to do. Unfortunately, for most adults it is not. Children do it, moving effortlessly from one total experience to another, but by the time you are grown, you have learned to bring into most situations the unnecessary baggage of previous incidents, present responsibilities, and future pursuits. Your restless and doubting mind pokes its interfering nose in when it need not, luring you into thoughts of the future, or of the past, or into analysis of your current actions so that you miss what is actually happening.

Getting There vs. Being Here. Generally people spend their lives in activity and rarely, if ever, take time out for contemplation, or to simply be in their own presence, unaffected by outside distractions.

Because so much of human behaviour is goal-oriented, people's attention is usually engaged in doing, with each action taken primarily to lead somewhere else. Actions then lose their intrinsic meaning — their only importance is to move you closer to your goal. But when you are truly being, you are not concerned with reaching somewhere else — you are already there.

For instance, a goal orientation in lovemaking makes orgasm the focus. When you are doing it rather than being it, there is an arbitrary separation between orgasm and 'all the other stuff'. The other stuff, although pleasurable, is second best, for unless you reach climax, what's the point? All other lovemaking activities are simply the sensual means to reach an orgasmic end. With this perspective, you deny yourself the potential of bliss that waits in every touch and caress. Tantric lovemaking, however, teaches you to realize that potential,, because being and doing become one.

The separation between the person doing the act and the act itself disappears — the dancer becomes the dance, meditation becomes contemplation, and lovers experience disappearance of all boundaries.

Tantric lovemaking is a wonderful way to enter into the contemplative state, because, not only is it a spiritual practice, it is also a source of great pleasure. In Tantra, we do not make love only because we yearn for spiritual awakening; we make love in order to 'make love'. Nor do we make love just to experience the thrill of orgasm — every moment of our sexual union is an end in itself, and by immersing ourselves in each moment, we experience connection with the Divine.

Secret 5 — Develop the Ability to Enjoy Pleasure

Our culture has trained us to believe that we don't really deserve pleasure, that cultivating pleasure is selfish, that giving it is more honourable than receiving it, and that having fun is wasting time — a distraction from more important matters.

When we do allow ourselves to receive pleasure, we give ourselves conditions such as, 'I should give him or her something in return for all this pleasure I am experiencing'; 'I am taking too much of his or her time'; or 'I shouldn't show how much I enjoy this'. Tantric sex helps you to develop the precious ability to be totally and unconditionally receptive to pleasure. The ability to become open and receive totally is a spiritual skill.

Ways to Develop the Ability to Enjoy Pleasure

Perceive without labelling. Paying attention to sensory information helps you learn to be fully present.

In this practice, you simply experience sensory phenomena; you do not analyse or even name what you are experiencing. Naming can set in motion a train of thought that pulls you out of the moment.

An example is listening to a bird's song. You may simply enjoy the lovely lilt of its call. Alternatively, you may hear it and start thinking, 'Oh what a lovely sound. That sounds like a beautiful dove. Isn't it great that there are doves nearby? I wonder if I can make a house for them so they will stay around? What kind of house would I make? Maybe the library has a book on birdhouses.'

Do the following sensory attention meditation three times a day. It is based on a one-minute meditation developed by Osho, the 20th century enlightened master from India.

* Stop whatever you are doing and become still.
* For one minute, pay attention to your senses: sight, smell, touch, taste, and hearing.
* Notice what is coming to you through your senses — simply smell the smell, hear the sound, and so on, without naming anything.

Make your Senses come Alive. This exercise helps to revive and stimulate senses other than sight.

* Gather items to help stimulate the senses of sound, touch, smell, and taste. Gather at least nine items for each sense, eg;

  Sound: chimes, drum, Tibetan singing bowl, whistle, music box, bell, rattle, metronome, pot lid and wooden spoon, recorded bird song, stiff fabric that rustles as you crinkle it in your hands, gong, flute, and so on.

Touch: feathers, silk, fur, warm oil, ice cubes, misting water bottle, powder, pumice stone, wooden massage roller, cotton balls, rough fabric (canvas, twill, homespun wool), leather, fleece, and others. Gather items to pass softly over your lover's skin, bare arms, neck, face, and so on.

Smell: essential oils, perfume, men's cologne, jars of spices, baby powder, fish sauce, coffee, aromatic flowers, and the like.

Taste: fruits (fresh or dried), chocolate, nuts, hot sauce, raw vegetables, liqueurs, crackers, cheeses, olives, pickles, and so on. These you will feed to your lover with your fingers and/or pass some tasty bits from your mouth to hers.

- Seat your lover in a comfortable chair and blindfold her.
- Help her to relax by breathing slowly and deeply together.
- Whisper softly into her ear something like this: 'With your permission, I am going to take you on a journey of sensory awakening. As I present you with each new item, allow yourself to experience it fully without trying to name or identify it.'
- Begin with the sense of sound. Make each sound for approximately 30 seconds. Take a 30 second break between sounds.
- Proceed to touch, then smell, and finally taste. Take a 30-second break between each sensory item in your repertoire.
- Go very slowly. Allow your partner plenty of time to experience each delightful sense. Be playful, loving, and respectful.
- Do this for each other on different days. If you want to take turns on the same day, use different items for each sense. This is also a marvellous exercise to do at a party.

Secret 6 — Discover Meditation

You may wonder what meditation has to do with sensuality and lovemaking.

In a nutshell, it provides clarity. It makes you total in the moment. It makes your mind focused. It makes your presence complete, and whole.

Imagine a bottle filled with sand and water. Shake it, and you can't distinguish a thing. This is the way the human mind functions during most of our normal, daily, waking life. It is processing so many thoughts, perceptions, and pieces of information that is continuously blurred. Often the circuits are jammed. But if you set the bottle down and leave it for a few minutes, the sand will arrange itself in harmonious layers on the bottom, and the water will become clear, In a way, meditation does the same.

By sitting in a position of relaxation and stillness, focusing your attention inside and deepening the rhythm of your breathing, the busy chatter of your thought processes gradually settles. As your mind quietness down, you will be able to direct more attention to your feelings and sensations, expanding your ability to experience pleasure.

In Spiritual Sex, meditation helps you bring heightened awareness to the body, heart and mind and to tune these three aspects of your being into a harmony that allows higher, more intense levels of pleasurable experience.

By meditation I mean a simple shift in focus — tuning in, turning within, relaxing, learning how to navigate beyond the chatter of the mind to expand your inner perceptions. Meditation in this sense is not an effort, but simply the conscious observation of what is happening inside.

Ways to meditate

Though there are hundreds of ways one can meditate, I give you some effective but simple techniques here.

Learning to Be Here Now. Try to bring into the rest of our lives the capacity for being in the moment that you find in Tantric love making.

There are simple tools — techniques common in meditative practices the world over — that you can use as you are learning to be here now.

You already have the equipment you need; all that is necessary is to put it into action. To become total in the moment, you can:

* Train your mind to focus on a mantra, a sound or an image — make it your servant, not your master.
* Get out of your head by going totally into your senses.
* Utilize the extraordinary power of breath. Practice one of the breathing techniques given earlier in this book.

Stop! What do you do while you are jogging, washing dishes, making love, and so on?

If your answer is anything other than jogging, washing dishes, or making love, you are not in the moment.

Try this exercise three times a day. When you are engaged in a particular activity, such as writing a report, playing catch with the kids, washing your car, weeding the garden, chopping wood, eating food, or hugging your mate, stop and ask yourself 'What am I doing? For example, while you are hugging your lover, ask, 'Am I doing anything in addition to hugging?' You may find that you are worrying, dreaming, or thinking about something else, talking about unrelated events, rushing to get out the door, and so on. If so, then you are likely missing out on the full sensual pleasure of your two bodies touching. You may miss the deep emotional connection that happens when you focus on opening to another, and you will not receive all the energetic nourishment that a hug could give you. As you practice pausing and asking, you will begin to recognize when you are really immersed in your activity and when you are distracted by other thoughts or actions.

Here and Now. This delightfully simple yet power-packed exercise is from Ram Dass' remarkable book *Be Here Now*. *Ask yourself:* Where am I? *Answer:* Here. *Ask yourself:* What time is it? *Answer:* Now. Say it until you can hear it.

Remind yourself during the day (at least three times) — with Post it notes or agenda items or programmable wristwatches — to stop and ask yourself the same questions and give yourself the same answers. 'Where am I?' 'Here.' 'What time is it?' 'Now.'

You will begin to understand that no matter where you are in the world, you are always here. No matter what the clock says, it is always now.

Life goes on, but you are here and now in the eternal present.

See for the Very First Time. One trap of memory is that you can end up making love to your recollection of your partner's body rather than to your living, breathing lover.

If you've made love many times before, you can assume that you know your partner's body perfectly — you know exactly the feel of her breasts or his buttocks, you are completely familiar with his scent. With Tantric lovemaking, even though you have touched that breast hundreds of times and think that you know it perfectly, you touch it, lick it, or suck it 'as if' for the first time.

Trick your mind into paying attention by pretending there will be a test later during which you'll be blindfolded and presented with a number of different breasts. From amongst them you will have to identify your lover's. How would you pay attention to that breast in order to identify it blindfolded? You would smell, taste, and touch very consciously, with highly focused attention — that is what experiencing as if for the very first time means. You won't need to employ this tactic after you have trained your mind to the attention habit.

Use Death as an Advisor. Your mind will pay close attention to what is happening if it believes this is the last time you will be experiencing something.

Use death as your advisor. Remind yourself that nothing is constant; you never know how much time you, or anyone else, has in this world. You may be kissing your lover for years to come, or the kiss you share this morning may be your last.

This is not fear tactic, but a way to help you transform a habit of inattention into the practice of mindfulness.

Backtrack. This exercise helps you catch yourself when your mind wants to wander off on an irrelevant train of thought. After repeating it a number of times, you will catch yourself quickly. Eventually the wandering happens less and less frequently and you will remain in the now moment more and more.

Focus your attention on any chosen object, for example, a plant in a pot. Try to pay attention only to the plant. At some point, you will notice that you are thinking about something completely unrelated to the plant. Stop as soon as you have become aware of your wandering thoughts and attempt to follow your thoughts back to their origin — the plant. For example while looking at the plant, you might have noticed the rich green colour of the leaves. This led you to the thought that the colour of the leaves would look great in the upstairs bedroom you are planning to repaint. There is a sale coming up at the carpet store and you could get a new carpet to go with the paint, but you're not sure your mate will agree to spend that much on the room. You wonder how much is left on the credit card or should you wait on the carpet, because you know you really need to get the brakes replaced on the car... At this point, you realize your mind has been wandering. Stop and recall each thought back to the start from replacing the brakes, to waiting on the carpet, to how much is left on the credit card, to your mate agreeing to spend that much money, to getting a carpet to match the green paint, to the sale at the carpet store, to painting the upstairs bedroom green, to the lovely green colour of the leaves of the plant.

Try to separate yourself from your thoughts and emotions by staying objective and impersonal in relation to them. This draws on your 'witness' consciousness, a part of you that can watch what you are thinking and feeling without need to judge or act. Imagine your mind is a movie screen and your thoughts are scenes passing by.

They come, they go, and no action is required.

Secret 7 — Allow Surrender within Yourself

Surrender is an essential aspect of the learning process in Tantra. There is, however, a lot of confusion about what surrender means. People are suspicious of this term, which they equate with loss of free will and personal power. In fact they are confusing surrender with submission, which is a passive attitude that implies giving up responsibility for one's behaviour — wanting someone else to do things for your. The word surrender has significant roots, on which 'render' has the meaning 'to melt', and 'sur' means 'super' or 'highest'. In other words, the true meaning of surrender is to melt into that which is higher than yourself.

In Tantric Sex you give yourself voluntarily to the highest aspect of your potential so that you can begin to grow into it. Understanding the art of surrender will make the experience of tantric sex much more available to you.

True surrender is a conscious choice made from free will. It means opening your heart and trusting the person you are with, whether it is your beloved or your teacher.

Ways to Practice Surrender

Drop Being in Control. People love to be in control; it makes them feel safe and secure. Very few are attracted to what may be perceived as its opposite — being out of control.

Being out of control can be scary, frustrating, even terrifying, and so people expend much time and energy trying to keep themselves, each other, and their environment under control. They develop many strategies, from the subtle to the blatant, to help feel they are in command, for example, keeping belongings and furnishings in precise order; maintaining strict schedules for waking, sleeping, and eating; making love in the one right place at the one right time in the one right position; or insisting on trying to win an argument whether their point is valid or not.

Control can also be a subtle dance of manipulation appearing in the guise of helpless need, or alternatively, as solicitous concern for others — making certain everything runs smoothly and all are happy; taking responsibility for everyone's well-being, so that ultimately everything is under control.

I see the opposite of control not as out of control, but rather as surrender or letting go.

Being in control is simply an illusion. When it comes right down to it, no one has absolute control over anything. You do however have a choice — you can choose to try and make things happen precisely as you want them to (and get frustrated when they do not turn out that way), or you can let go, surrendering to the ebb and flow of life.

Surrender. Surrender is essential for crating love and for spiritual union. Perhaps you are afraid of surrender because you equate surrender with submission, but the two are very different. Submission exists in the context of power in relationships; it implies domination. Someone submits when they are overpowered or overwhelmed, but surrender is not submission, nor is it passivity, losing, or being inferior. Surrender is an active process of conscious, courageous choice, because although you are not submitting, you do have to give something up. Your ego knows and fears this. Your ego likes things as they are. If some change is required, it wants to take credit — to feel the pride of accomplishment and success. But in the spiritual quest, you give up this self-importance. You give up the claim 'I did it on my own, my way'.

The fear of surrendering can be so strong that you may feel as if you will be diminished, even annihilated — you will disappear. The actuality is very different. Instead of diminishing you, surrender makes you bigger, expanding and connecting you to something so much greater than your ego could ever have imagined.

If surrender is not giving up, giving in, or being dominated, what is it? It is:

Trusting that there is a larger life process that you are part of and can be in alignment with.

Showing vulnerability, admitting even that you do not know what to do when you feel fear and insecurity.

Making choices and taking risks — acting in spite of your fear and insecurity.

Letting go of attachment to the results of your choices.

Suspending judgement when things do not go the way you want them to.

Being open to surprises — allowing that there may be more possibilities than you thought or could have imagined, and that these may be better, not worse, than what you wanted.

As you begin to explore the meaning of surrender, in terms of actual behaviour, you will come to a critical distinction. On the one hand, there are those things in your life that you make happen, that you take from life, or that you achieve with willpower and as the result of acquired talent. There are others that come to you as gifts from out of the mystery, the Universe, or from God, wonderful surprises, beyond anything you could have imagined, better than you could have planned or even hoped for.

Let Go of Results. Surrendering means you maintain your intention and you dive in whole-heartedly, but you let go of any expectation that things will turn out the way you planned or expected.

When you let go of the attachment to end results, you disconnect from the typical emotional overreaction that occurs when things do not turn out as expected. You do not have to worry about the precise outcome beforehand. You do not have to be angry or depressed if it does not turn out your way. You cannot fake this detachment, but you can be aware of your emotions (for example worry, fear, and anger.) When you feel negative emotions rising, you can use emotional release techniques to help let them go. It is easier to detach from expectations when you do not suppress or deny your emotions, but instead let them out in constructive ways, like letting off the steam in a boiler.

When you let go of attachment to a particular outcome, you allow yourself to be open to the surprise of something other than what you wanted. You acknowledge that what is coming could be better than you had imagined, rather than uselessly indulging yourself in the fear that it will be worse. Certain positive effects appear in your life quickly when you let go of all concern for a particular outcome. For example, your stress level from worry drops off sharply, you can make better decisions, and you act more efficiently when you can stay emotionally calm, even when things do not seem to be going your way.

When you surrender and let go of any expectations about what the results of your actions will be, you will come to understand that even when things seem to go badly, in the longer perspective, these seeming setbacks lead to larger outcomes that are extraordinary and filled with unanticipated delight.

Instead of losing some imaginary freedom, this way of living offers you true freedom. You can do anything you want, but of course, as an aware human being, you will not do just anything at all. On the contrary, you will consistently act in ways that are seemingly 'right' as you move to higher levels of self-actualization. You will know the meaning of abundance and share it freely with others. Your optimism and comfort in yourself will radiate. People will feel good to be around you.

You cannot fake surrender; you cannot pretend to give up expectation. You must simply jump into the abyss, in faith and trust.

Let Go in Relationship. What causes the relationship to sink is the accumulated weight of unresolved 'stuff'. In relationships, letting go means to reveal the emotional truth of what is going on inside you. Vulnerable emotions are usually the fear and insecurity that lie below anger. In this you are taking a risk — the other person could reject, judge, or take advantage of you. It means revealing your limitations and weaknesses, which may be as simple as admitting you don't know how to do something or you don't have the solution to a problem.

Revealing emotional vulnerabilities in a loving relationship will deliver immediate benefits in your life.

You give your partner permission to take off the mask of infallibility and perfection.

Your lover will be much more inclined to show you affection if you are vulnerable. Unbending strength is unapproachable, while being vulnerable is an invitation to intimacy. I am not talking about whining and complaining, or false modesty, but being true about your limitations and your capabilities. Revealing your vulnerabilities is not a strategy to seduce someone, but an honest, open attempt at real intimacy.

Now, one last secret for those of you who wish to become masters at the art and practice of pleasure. I have mentioned earlier in the book that the master of Tantra is a master of his tongue! He is also a master of his hands. After the tongue, the hands are the most powerful and dexterous tools available to you to give pleasure to your partner. Learn the skills of massage and sensitive touch, and you will never leave your partner dissatisfied or un-fulfiled in your lovemaking.

Erotic Massage

Primarily for arousal, erotic massage focuses on tantalizing skin-to-skin contact that becomes increasingly sexual as the massage continues. Using light, feathery touches, begin moving inwards from the extremities of your lover's body, for example from her toes, up her feet, to calves and thighs, stopping just short of her genitals, or her fingers to palms to inner elbows to armpits and almost to her nipples, Only slowly, as her body awakens under your teasing touch do you move on to actually caress her hot sexual spots.

With erotic massage you may use not only your hands but also your tongue, lips, hair, or other exotic aids such as feathers and even ice cubes. Add more spice with a blindfold or by loosely binding your lover's wrists and ankles to the bed corners so she is at your tender mercy.

Perineum Massage

The perineum, that small patch of skin between a man's anus and scrotum or between a woman's anus and vagina, is a powerful point of pleasure that is often overlooked. Lightly tapping, pressing, or massaging it during lovemaking can be highly arousing.

For a man who is learning ejaculation mastery, massaging the perineum regularly is essential to help him move accumulated sexual energy away from the genitals where it can cause discomfort. Begin by pressing on the perineum, back towards the anus where you will feel a small indentation — this is the 'P-spot', for prostate glands. The prostate feels like a firm lump about the size of a large grape or a small walnut.

Gently push and probe the entire area with your fingertips. Especially delightful is massaging the perineum in circular motions, first clockwise and then counterclockwise, with a piece of folded silk (two layers). Either you or your lover should do a prostate massage after every lovemaking session. Or you can add it as part of your continual loving touch during sacred sex. You can also massage the prostate directly through the anus.

Yoni Massage

The Yoni Massage or female genital massage, brings whole-body healing and emotional opening. Your intention is not arousal, or orgasm, although these may well occur, but rather to help your lover become more sensitive, relaxed, and connected to her yoni — her sacred temple. Much frustration, pain, and trauma are held in the tissues of the vagina and loving massage can help discharge them. This process may bring up strong emotions — feelings of fear or anxiety and joyous outpourings of release. It may take several sessions before her yoni has healed so that she can fully enjoy the range of sexual pleasures it holds.

* Your lover lies on her back, a towel-covered pillow under her hips.
* Her legs are apart, knees slightly bent. Sit between her legs.
* Look into each other's eyes and breathe slowly and deeply together.
* Gently massage her legs, belly, and torso, advancing without haste to her inner thighs and pelvis.
* When she is relaxed, move to her yoni, and, asking permission to honour this most sacred spot, pour a good quality, water-based lubricant on her mound and begin to massage it slowly. 'Slowly' is a key point for this entire massage.
* Gently squeezing each outer lip between thumb and forefinger, stroke up and down.
* Ask her to tell you if she wants more pressure or speed or softness.

* Repeat the stroking, squeezing motion on her inner lips. Move to her clitoris, circling, squeezing, and gently pulling.
* When you feel she is ready, ask permission to enter her enchanted garden and gently insert your finger — some women may prefer two fingers.
* Crook your finger in a 'come hither' motion and press it against the walls just inside the entrance of her vaginal canal.
* Explore all around this wonderful opening, fraction of an inch fraction of an inch.
* If you encounter spots that are painful or tight, stop movement but continue to press your finger there.
* Breathe together. You may notice tingling or heat as the tension releases.
* Move in a little deeper and again press all around.
* This is the area of the G-spot, which can be extremely sensitive — its spongy tissue is sometimes a storehouse of sexual frustration and pain — so move respectfully.
* Some women feel a burning or a desire to urinate when the G-spot is awakened; continue to apply pressure and allow the sensation to pass.
* Move deeper still, straightening your finger and pressing along the sides as you go farther back toward the cervix.
* Wherever she feels trauma or pain, stop movement, press the spot firmly, and breathe deeply, until there is a release.
* If your lover would like you to, as you continue your internal massage, begin to stimulate her clitoris with your other hand awakening her to a state of high arousal.
* She may experience orgasm — clitorally or vaginally or in combination.
* When she feels she has had enough, slowly take your hands away. Complete your massage by gently holding her in your loving arms.

Lingam Massage

Men, too, need gentle healing of their genitals — a purging of emotional and energetic blockages. When a man holds frustration and hurts in his genital region, the muscles can be tight, affecting his capacity for erection and his ability to master ejaculation.

The lingam massage relaxes these tense muscles and helps a man open to his receptive side so he may experience deeper levels of pleasure. If the massage brings up strong emotions for your lover, encourage him to allow them out.

* Your lover lies on his back, a towel-covered pillow under his hips.
* His legs are apart, knees slightly bent. Sit between his legs.
* Look into each other's eyes and breathe slowly and deeply together.
* Gently massage his legs, belly and torso, advancing without haste to his inner thighs and pelvis.
* Ask permission to honour his lingam, his 'want of light', and with a quality lubricant, deeply massage the muscles at the top of his inner thighs, in the crease where his legs and pelvic floor meet. Work along the connecting bone and muscles, releasing tension as you go. 'Slowly' is a key point for this entire massage.
* Ask him to tell you when he wants more or less pressure or a change of stroke or to touch a different spot.
* Massage above his lingam on the pubic bone.
* Move down to the scrotum, gently kneading and pulling his testicles.
* Pay special attention to the perineum, circling and pushing the tissues.
* Bring your loving touch to his lingam, stroking the shaft with varying pressure and speed. With alternating hands slide up from the base of the shaft to the head and then off. Repeat

this movement and then reverse direction — slide from the top down.

* Hold his lingam by its head and gently shake it back and forth.
* Thoroughly massage the head of his lingam.
* He may or may not get an erection. If he does, it may come and go throughout your massage.
* If he feels he is coming close to ejaculation, slow down or stop your massaging, or move to a different spot, for instance the perineum. Breathe deeply together.
* Move from perineum to testicles to lingam and back again, paying attention to different areas as he rises to a peak, and then backs off. The lingam massage is a great aid to learning ejaculation mastery.
* Perhaps he would like to ejaculate at the end of the massage or he may want to retain his sexual energy. Whatever his preference, when he feels he has had enough, remove your hands slowly and reverently. He may want you to hold him in your arms to complete your session.

Here are also some simple suggestions for you to keep in mind as you begin to live life the tantric way.

Some Final Simple Soulful-Sex Suggestions

Tantra, sacred sex, is a practical key to unlocking your potential for an intimate, passionate relationship.

The approaches and exercises you have just read about in this book can bring great meaning to your life. All that's required now is some effort on your part. It doesn't take much extra time, just a little discipline — and you'll soon see a noticeable difference.

To receive the maximum benefits you deserve, I suggest you take the following steps as well. They will likely require some shifts in attitudes and behaviours, but you, your partner, and your relationship are worth it!

* On your own, and with your partner, examine your beliefs about sexuality, spirituality, and relationships. Replace unwanted negative messages with supportive, positive ones.
* Make your relationship a top priority and set your actions accordingly. This means feeding your union with time and commitment. Do it despite all the other things crying out for your attention and you'll see that a loving relationship helps all else flow more smoothly.
* Connect in an intimate, loving way with your partner daily.
* At least once per week have a two-to-four-hour Tantra date and experiment with the marvellous processes described in this book. During that time, allow and encourage your sexuality to be more than physical.

  Give yourself freely and fully to your lover and the Divine, despite your fears.

  Share your body and your heart. Tame your mind. Unite your spirits.
* Keep pushing your envelope, the limits of your awareness, playfully, respectfully, and boldly. Always have faith in your capacity to create together the passionate, intimate life you want.

Tantric Meditation 7

Nourishing the Positive Pole

This meditation is based on an unusual method that Shiva gives to Shakti in *Vigyan Bhairav* Tantra. It is unusual because the original method is designed exclusively for women.

Shiva says: 'Feel the fine qualities of creativity permeating your breasts and assuming delicate configurations.' This is something that women can try on their own.

* Sitting silently in meditation, bring your attention to your breasts. In the beginning, it may also be helpful to lightly caress them, with eyes closed, to help sensitize them. It can be helpful, too, to use your breath and imagination: as you breathe in, imagine that you are filling your breasts with energy and light.
* Slowly, you will begin to feel a sensation of soft sweetness in your breasts. This is the energy that becomes a mother's love for her child. It is not only milk that a baby receives from the breast; it is love — the purest form of nourishment. In this way, you are giving yourself the nourishment that normally would be given to a baby.
* There is nothing more to do. Simply enjoy and receive the energy that you are creating by yourself. Then, when you have finished, lie down quietly and rest with eyes closed for about fifteen minutes.
* It is not possible for men to have the same experience at the breasts, because men and women have different energy polarities;

at the breasts a woman's energy is positive, while a man's is negative.

* At the centre, a man's energy is positive while a woman's is negative. Men can have a similar experience by focusing their attention in the same way on the sex centre.
* Follow the same instructions: with eyes closed, lightly caress your genitals, using your breath to fill them with love. Stay relaxed, soft and gentle, letting the light and the love energy fill your pelvic region and expand through your whole body.
* When you feel filled with light, lie down quietly and rest with eyes closed for about fifteen minutes.

Appendices

1. Sexual Beliefs Questionnaire

These statements about sexuality are intended to help you become aware of your own and your partner's beliefs, assumptions, and attitudes about sex. The purpose is not to categorize you, judge you, or make you feel either good or bad.

This is an exercise in sexual self-awareness. If you already have a sex-positive consciousness, you are fortunate indeed. That will make it much easier for you to progress rapidly in the use of Tantra as a spiritual practice. If you discover that you are carrying the weight of a sex-negative consciousness, you are presented with a challenge and an opportunity at the same time. Your challenge is discovering how to let go of your negative conditioning. Remember, recognition is a step on the road toward change. Your opportunity is to mature spiritually as a whole human being, to celebrate life in a body that is the holy temple of your soul. In this maturity, you can learn to give and receive love sexually, to surrender to your lover, to experience your birthright of bliss.

Sex-Positive Statements

Statements	Agree	Disagree	No Opinion
1. Sex is good, healthy, and normal.	☐	☐	☐
2. Sex is important or essential in my life.	☐	☐	☐
3. Sex is a source of pleasure and meaning in my life.	☐	☐	☐
4. It is good to talk frankly about sex with children, at whatever age they show interest.	☐	☐	☐
5. Male and female naked bodies are beautiful.	☐	☐	☐
6. Women can be just as sexual as men.	☐	☐	☐
7. Sex can continue happily well into old age.	☐	☐	☐
8. Sex can be a meditation.	☐	☐	☐
9. Sex can be a spiritual practice.	☐	☐	☐
10. Sex can be sacred and holy.	☐	☐	☐
11. Through sex, it is possible to have a mystical or religious experience.	☐	☐	☐
12. Masturbation is normal and healthy.	☐	☐	☐
13. Anal sex is normal and healthy.	☐	☐	☐
14. It does not matter what a person's sexual orientation is.	☐	☐	☐
15. We openly show affection by hugging, kissing, and touching when we are around our children.	☐	☐	☐
16. Our sex life continues to evolve.	☐	☐	☐
17. I have fun with sex.	☐	☐	☐
18. I can be creative in sex.	☐	☐	☐
19. I am confident with myself as a lover.	☐	☐	☐
20. I have sex frequently.	☐	☐	☐

21. I love to try new sexual techniques and do so often.	☐	☐	☐
22. We experiment with different locations for sex.	☐	☐	☐
23. We have tried using a variety of sex toys.	☐	☐	☐
24. We sometimes watch erotic or sex instruction videos together.	☐	☐	☐
25. I have read at least one sex-instruction book since high school.	☐	☐	☐
26. I have taken steps and made efforts to understand more about sexuality since high school.	☐	☐	☐
27. The idea of extending lovemaking for hours is appealing.	☐	☐	☐
28. I try to come to our lovemaking well rested, calm, and relaxed.	☐	☐	☐
29. I open my heart to my partner during lovemaking.	☐	☐	☐
30. Sex is a way that I join with my partner on much more than a physical level.	☐	☐	☐
31. I sometimes laugh or cry with joy during or after sex.	☐	☐	☐
32. I regularly communicate with my partner about what I like and dislike sexually.	☐	☐	☐
33. I pay wonderful attention to my partner's responses when we make love.	☐	☐	☐
34. Our lovemaking includes much more than intercourse.	☐	☐	☐
35. Our lovemaking sometimes lasts more than one hour.	☐	☐	☐
36. We share being active and passive partners — givers and receivers of pleasure and initiators of sex.	☐	☐	☐

37. Do not usually touch my partner's genitals until she is very highly aroused and well lubricated. ☐ ☐ ☐
38. I usually wait until she has come close to or has had an orgasm before vaginal penetration. ☐ ☐ ☐
39. Masturbation is a good way for me to learn about what I like sexually. ☐ ☐ ☐
40. I masturbate for my lover. ☐ ☐ ☐
41. It turns me on to see my lover masturbate. ☐ ☐ ☐
42. I reach orgasm quite easily through masturbation. ☐ ☐ ☐
43. I regularly experience orgasm during lovemaking with my partner. ☐ ☐ ☐
44. I experience different types of orgasm. ☐ ☐ ☐
45. I make lots of sound during sex. ☐ ☐ ☐
46. I enjoy giving oral sex. ☐ ☐ ☐
47. I enjoy receiving oral sex. ☐ ☐ ☐
48. We have experimented with anal sex. ☐ ☐ ☐
49. I'm open to the idea that anal sex can be pleasurable. ☐ ☐ ☐
50. We frequently open our eyes during lovemaking, and look into each other's eyes. ☐ ☐ ☐

The more of these statements you agree to, the more sex-positive are your attitudes, beliefs, and assumptions about sex. If you agree with many or most of these statements, you are probably comfortable being in a body and with your sexuality. You are well informed and have considerable knowledge and skill of sexual technique and style. Your sexuality is likely integrated within the context of your relationship and your entire life. Sex for you is fun, healthy, normal, and possibly even sacred. You are able to give and receive pleasure, surrendering to your lover, and letting go of the need to be in control during lovemaking.

Sex-Negative Statements

Almost everyone will answer yes to some of these negative statements. This should not be of concern to you assuming you answered yes to many more of the sex-positive statements. The opportunity is for you to become aware of any strong sex-negative bias.

You will have to decide what your answers mean by looking inside of yourself. Once you are aware of a powerful sex-negative bias, you can take steps to change it — if you want to. This book offers many ways for you to transform a sex-negative bias into a joyous celebration of spiritual sexuality.

Sex-Negative Statements

Statements	Agree	Disagree	No Opinion
1. Sex is bad, abnormal, unhealthy, dangerous, dirty, or a sin.	☐	☐	☐
2. Sex outside of marriage is a sin.	☐	☐	☐
3. Sex without love is bad; only sex with love is acceptable.	☐	☐	☐
4. Sex is acceptable only in order to have children.	☐	☐	☐
5. It is okay for men to like sex, but not for women to like sex.	☐	☐	☐
6. Men cannot control themselves when it comes to sex.	☐	☐	☐
7. It is the woman's responsibility to avoid provoking men's interest in sex. If a woman looks, talks, or acts sexy, she is just asking for it.	☐	☐	☐
8. Good girls do not show interest in sex.	☐	☐	☐
9. Mothers should not act, talk, dress, dance, or be sexy.	☐	☐	☐
10. Women should not initiate sex; only men should initiate sex.	☐	☐	☐

11. Sex is just a physical thing.	☐	☐	☐
12. Truly spiritual people are not very interested in sex; if they do have sexual interest they sublimate it.	☐	☐	☐
13. Homosexuality is bad or a sin.	☐	☐	☐
14. Anal sex is bad or a sin.	☐	☐	☐
15. Masturbation is bad or a sin.	☐	☐	☐
16. Masturbation is second best to 'real' sex.	☐	☐	☐
17. A woman should never use a vibrator.	☐	☐	☐
18. Sex is a duty.	☐	☐	☐
19. I am uncomfortable touching, hugging, and kissing in front of my children, parents, family, and friends.	☐	☐	☐
20. I do not like my body.	☐	☐	☐
21. I worry about what my lover thinks about my body.	☐	☐	☐
22. I feel threatened, afraid, insecure, or inadequate if my lover wants sex frequently.	☐	☐	☐
23. I am embarrassed to make sounds during sex.	☐	☐	☐
24. I use sex to bargain for what I want.	☐	☐	☐
25. I withhold sex to show disapproval or to punish my lover.	☐	☐	☐
26. The idea of extending lovemaking for hours turns me off.	☐	☐	☐
27. I would be embarrassed to invite God into my bedroom while I am having sex.	☐	☐	☐

The more of these statements you agree with, the more repressed is your sexuality. You probably do not enjoy sex and are likely to avoid it if possible. During sex, you may feel shame, guilt, and fear. For you sex is purely physical, lacking any spiritual dimension. You may use sex manipulatively to get what you want or as a weapon to be in control.

Sexual History: Negative Sexual Experiences from Your Past

Statements	Agree	Disagree	No Opinion
1. Sex was rarely openly discussed in my family.	☐	☐	☐
2. One or both of my parents taught me that sex was bad or a sin.	☐	☐	☐
3. There was little or no physical affection in my family.	☐	☐	☐
4. According to my religion or the religion I was raised with, sex is bad or is a sin, except within marriage, and then is primarily for procreation.	☐	☐	☐
5. I received little or no sex education in school.	☐	☐	☐
6. Sex education in school left me with the impression that sex was bad, dangerous, dirty, or a sin.	☐	☐	☐
7. Sex education in grade school or high school left me with the impression that sex was okay for males, but not okay for females.	☐	☐	☐
8. Men's naked bodies are ugly or shameful.	☐	☐	☐
9. Women's naked bodies are ugly or shameful.	☐	☐	☐
10. The longer we can delay having children learn about sex, the better.	☐	☐	☐
11. The idea that my children would hear the sounds I make during sex is unacceptable.	☐	☐	☐
12. I feel shame or guilt when I think about or have sex.	☐	☐	☐
13. I become afraid when I think about or have sex.	☐	☐	☐

14. I sometimes cry with sadness during or after sex.	☐	☐	☐
15. I can remember at least one experience of sexual abuse, sexual trauma, or being forced to have sex against my will.	☐	☐	☐

The more of these statements you agree with, the more likely you are to carry a burden of sex-negative conditioning from home, school, and/or church. There was probably little discussion of sexuality at home, and the message you received from school (and/or church) was that sex was to be avoided. You may have experienced: sexual abuse or sexual trauma. You may avoid sex, or paradoxically you could be promiscuous.

Sexual Knowledge and Skill

Statements	Agree	Disagree	No Opinion
1. Our lovemaking typically lasts less than 30 minutes.	☐	☐	☐
2. Our sex usually begins and ends at the genitals; there is little or no foreplay.	☐	☐	☐
3. Our sex has become routine or boring.	☐	☐	☐
4. Our sex has become primarily a release of tension.			
5. Sex not complete without intercourse.	☐	☐	☐
6. Having an orgasm is the goal of sex.	☐	☐	☐
7. Ejaculation is usually involuntary for me.	☐	☐	☐
8. Our sex typically ends abruptly with the man's ejaculation. We rarely cuddle after that. We usually go to sleep or get up to do something else.	☐	☐	☐
9. I sometimes fake orgasms.	☐	☐	☐
10. We almost always have our eyes closed during lovemaking.	☐	☐	☐
11. I do not tell my lover what I like and do not like.	☐	☐	☐
12. My lover should know what I want.	☐	☐	☐
13. I do not know how to turn my partner on.	☐	☐	☐
14. I would like to learn more about sex techniques but I am afraid to admit it.	☐	☐	☐
15. I learned what I need to know about sexual anatomy and sexual techniques in grade school or high school.	☐	☐	☐
16. Sex should just come naturally; planning for it or learning about it makes it artificial.	☐	☐	☐
17. Sex should happen only in the bedroom, in bed.	☐	☐	☐

18. We rarely experiment with different positions during intercourse; usually it is man on top.	☐	☐	☐
19. I do not know how to touch my partner sexually.	☐	☐	☐
20. I do not know where the G-spot is.	☐	☐	☐
21. I do not know what the prostate does.	☐	☐	☐
22. I do not know where the prostate is.	☐	☐	☐
23. Delaying ejaculation is dangerous for a man's sexual health.	☐	☐	☐
24. The only reasons a man loses his erection are because he has ejaculated or because he is suffering from erectile dysfunction.	☐	☐	☐
25. Sex after menopause rapidly drops off.	☐	☐	☐
26. People are not interested in sex after age 60.	☐	☐	☐
27. People are not capable of sex after age 90.	☐	☐	☐
28. Only really beautiful, young people have fabulous sex lives.	☐	☐	☐
29. I cannot imagine why anyone would want to extend lovemaking for hours.	☐	☐	☐
30. Tantra is just a cult.	☐	☐	☐
31. Tantra is just disguised indulgence.	☐	☐	☐

The more of these statements you agree with, the less satisfying your experience with sex likely is. You need more knowledge and skill to create a consistently fulfiling sex life. You entertain some common misconceptions about sex. You may not think sex is bad, but it may well be a duty or obligation, or a simple stress or tension release, rather than a source of pleasure or a spiritual practice. If you are a woman, you may have difficulty having orgasm. If you are a man, you may have performance anxiety and feelings of inadequacy about pleasing your partner. You may ejaculate prematurely.

2. Energy Exercises With Your Partner

You may have experienced a sexual encounter that was physically satisfying, even satiating, but that nonetheless left you feeling very separate form your lover and internally empty. Although your bodies joined, your essential selves did not — there was no energetic bond, no joining of hearts and souls. Tantric lovemaking takes you beyond connecting your physical bodies to connecting your energetic bodies and ultimately to connection with the cosmic life force or God.

These are a couple of exercises for connecting energetically with another in a non-sexual way. Knowing how to do this when you are unaroused makes it easier to do so during the heat of lovemaking.

1. Hands to Heart

Stand facing your partner, feet solidly on the floor, shoulder-width apart. Knees are slightly bent. Back is straight but not rigid. There are four sections to this exercise:

* Vigorously rub your hands together, building energy in them. Feel this charge, your life force, in and around your hands. With palms facing toward you, slowly bring your hands, with their powerful energy, toward your heart. Notice when you start to feel the energy approaching.
* Now begin to rock your pelvis back and forth and breathe rhythmically as you rock. Again, rub your hands together and bring them towards your heart. Notice when you start to feel the energy approaching. Is there a difference from the first time?

* Continuing pelvic rocking, match your breathing rhythm to your partner's. Rub your hands together again. Move your hands, palms forward, toward your partner's hands. When do you feel contact?
* Continue breathing in unison and rocking your pelvis. Charge your hands again. This time direct your hands toward each other's hearts. Notice when you make contact with your partner. Notice when you feel his approaching energy touch you. Be aware of and considerate toward sensory perceptions and emotions that may come up for each of you as you do this exercise. Let them flow freely. You might he drawn physically toward each other, for a hug, or you may feel the need to be very separate. Listen and do what feels right, without analysing or judging.

2. Merging

* Stand facing your partner with enough space between you that you both feel distinct from each other.
* Your feet are solidly on the floor, shoulder-width apart. Knees are slightly bent. Back is straight but not rigid. Your eyes are closed.
* Put your attention in your backbone. Feel the individual discs and bones. Feel your spine as a complete unit. Are there parts you cannot sense? Accept that without judging yourself.
* Gather your energy along your backbone. Picture it forming into a pillar that extends from your head down into the Earth. What sensations are you aware of?
* When your pillar of energy feels relatively steady, open your eyes. What happens when you look at your partner? Does your energy flow out toward her? If it does not on its own, consciously send it. Picture it moving from your back forward to join with her energy.
* Shut your eyes. Pull your energy back again into your supporting pillar along your backbone. Hold it there for a count of five.
* This time as you open your eyes, concentrate on holding your energy in its pillar for five more seconds.
* Now, let it go to unite with your partner's energy.

* Once again, shut your eyes and pull your energy back to form a stable pillar.
* Repeat this process five more times, endeavouring to hold your separate pillar and your merged energies a few seconds longer each time.
* If you want to, make sounds as you are merging and separating.
* On the last reforming of your energy pillar, keep looking into your partner's eyes.
* Finish with a hug if you like
* Do this merging exercise again, this time while doing pelvic rocking and breathing in harmony together.
* Perform six repetitions of gathering energy along your spine then sending it forward to join with your partner's energy.
* End with a hug if you like.

What differences were you aware of when doing this exercise standing still and doing it rocking? Was one easier than the other? Was one more powerful?

3. The Eye-gazing Technique

Eye gazing is a basic Tantric sex practice, widely taught by Tantra teachers of all schools of thought. It's a fundamental practice that leads to intense experiences when you do it right. It sounds so simple — looking at each others eyes — but in fact, think about how difficult it can be to actually look into anyone's eyes for any amount of time. Fears of intimacy can make it even more uncomfortable to look into a lover's eyes deeply for an extended period of time. How do you feel when a lover looks deeply and directly in your eyes? You might be delighted, but you might also feel vulnerable, self-conscious, or embarrassed. These feelings are normal!

Eye gazing in Tantric sex practice means looking deeply into your partner's eyes, to see behind the obvious (eye colour, eyelashes, expression) into his or her soul. It can be challenging and takes practice.

Eye gazing is extremely effective and valuable because...

* It stills your mind and focuses your attention on what you are doing rather than on distracting thoughts, to keep you present and in the moment.
* It gives your partner a good feeling that you're totally paying attention and are present for him or her.
* It enables you to confront your fears of deep connection with your beloved.
* It transforms your relationship to each other by getting beyond mental distractions and physical judgements to enter each other's soul.

It's true that when people first fall in love, they often spend extended periods gazing into each other's eyes. In practising and perfecting eye gazing you are consciously re-creating the experience of falling in love.

To do eye gazing, stand facing your partner in a relaxed and open posture and gaze softly into each other's eyes for at least three minutes. (You can also do eye gazing while sitting in *yab-yum* or any comfortable position as long as your energy centres are aligned.) Look predominantly into each other's left (receiving) eye. Remember it's not a staring contest; keep your eyes relaxed and blink if you have to. Come back to gazing if you get distracted. Instead of focusing on the outward act of looking, be receptive so you can melt deeper and deeper into the union with your beloved.

Notice whatever feelings come up (fear, embarrassment, attraction, love). Keep breathing. Notice your body's reactions (lips tightening, squinting, coughing, and shifting). Eventually you will be able to keep more still.

4. Seven Chakra Meditation

Imagine you are lying in the sun. Feel the heat on your body and allow the light to permeate your cells. As your cells absorb heat and light, they begin to awaken and come alive. Allow your body to become transparent, like clear glass, as you allow the light to penetrate to the core of your being. Maintain your focused attention for five minutes or longer depending upon whether this exercise is working for you.

Try to actually see your aura, or imagine your aura if you cannot actually see it, surrounding your body in a rainbow of vibrating, undulating colours. You will now shift your attention from one chakra to the next, pausing at each for at least two minutes, or longer if that feels right for you. With your attention focused on each chakra, put your left hand on the chakra, and at the same time hold your right hand over your body at that point but not touching. Rotate your right hand in a clockwise direction. At each chakra, imagine the colour of light that is associated with that chakra, and imagine that light is cleansing, clearing, healing, and balancing the energy of that chakra. As you breathe in, life energy follows your breath to the chakra you are touching. As you exhale, any negative or excess energy flows out with the breath. Imagine that the chakra begins to spin in a clockwise direction.

* *First Chakra/Root Chakra:* The light here is a sensual subdued red. Feel yourself solidly grounded to Mother Earth. Repeat the affirmation, 'I am calm, safe, and secure. My body is a divine temple for experiencing this world.'

* *Second Chakra/Belly Chakra:* The light here is a deep saturated orange. Repeat the affirmation, 'I am strong and confident. I am comfortable in my body. My body is beautiful. I enjoy a healthy, passionate sexuality. I am easily orgasmic.'
* *Third Chakra/Solar Plexus Chakra:* The colour here is a bright yellow. Repeat the affirmation, 'I am fully alive. I can feel everything. I love life and can create results that are important to me. I regularly experience success in the things I try.'
* *Fourth Chakra/Heart Chakra:* The colour here is a deep, saturated green, the rich green of new life in springtime. Feel the warmth of love flowing in and out of your open heart, nourishing you as it flows in and nourishing the world as it flows out. Repeat this affirmation, 'I am love. I give and receive love easily and unconditionally. Love is the reason I am in this body.'
* *Fifth Chakra/Throat Chakra:* The colour here is blue, a pale blue as the sky or a dark, saturated blue as the sky reflected off water. Repeat this affirmation, 'I am confident in speaking my truth. The truth sets me free.'
* *Sixth Chakra/Third Eye Chakra:* The colour here is a deep, saturated dark blue. Imagine a third eye at the centre of your forehead opening. As it opens, you are able to see and understand the meaning of all things. Repeat this affirmation, 'I have access to wisdom and always know the right thing to do in every situation because I understand what things mean and what they are for. I act so that everyone will benefit.'
* *Seventh Chakra:* Concentrate on the colour white, the purest, finest white imaginable, or alternatively the absolute clarity of a perfect diamond. Repeat this affirmation, 'I am one with God. I am an enlightened being. Cosmic light, energy, intelligence, and wisdom flow through my body, mind, and heart. I am one with my beloved.'

5. The 10 Questions of Good Sex

* What do you like?
* Does that feel good?
* Show me what you like?
* Do you like that?
* Harder?
* Softer?
* What don't you like and why?
* What's your favourite position and why?
* Slower?
* Faster?

6. A Nine Day Tantric Love Session

This is a nine-day Tantric session designed to be practised by a couple who are self-disciplined, and dedicated and devoted to each other. This technique was practiced by advanced practitioners in the ancient schools of Tantra.

There is to be no penis penetration until the third night.

The idea is to get to know, become familiar with, each other as people, and as the goddess and god within each other.

In addition, to take time to appreciate each other's physical beauty or other qualities without sexual overtones.

The first evening, depending on the weather, dress lightly without any constricting garments, and go for a walk.

Holding hands lightly is good, but if not then an occasional touch is recommended.

Enjoy the warm or cool evening air, the smells and sounds, together, breathe deeply, but be aware of each other, the presence, feel the joy of being with her or him, and allow the scents and sounds to enhance that.

Let him or her know how you feel about your partner — quietly and sincerely.

Don't make a big thing of it, but express the genuine awareness of the privilege of being with her or him.

Talk, quietly, ask non-intrusive questions about the other person, go deeper into interesting aspects but immediately drop anything which the other person is reluctant or even hesitant to discuss.

After an hour find a restaurant and have a light meal — no meat or alcohol on this occasion.

The idea is not to focus on the food but to continue to enjoy each other's presence in a slightly different environment.

Return to the place where you intend to spend the night together.

After a while go to bed, undress each other slowly, appreciating your partner's body, then lay naked, talk occasionally, touch each other lightly — face, arms, body, but avoiding the breasts and genitals.

When you are ready, cuddle each other but do not fondle, then sleep either in each other's arms or with at least one part of the body, a hand or foot, touching the other.

(During the walk, the meal, and when you return, drop your defenses with each other; talk openly and freely, but nothing that will hurt the other — no sexual jokes or erotic fantasies during the first evening).

The next day begins with bathing together, then breakfast, it can be fun making it together. Light kissing is now permitted.

You are handling your partner as you would a delicate and beautiful flower.

After breakfast lay on the bed naked, or in very light covering, touching and talking.

Continue to do this, with breaks to eat light meals or perhaps get dressed and go for a short walk, then return, undress and continue touching and caressing, and talking.

The idea of touching is to imagine it is your own face or arm you are stroking and caressing, so that you are also experiencing what your partner is experiencing, as she or he does the same with you. You are creating empathy with each other, an intimate closeness, and getting away from the nervousness of unfamiliarity. You are now familiar with each other's body and over the embarrassment, if any, of being naked with another person.

The night is exactly the same as the previous night, except now you can both express how much you can appreciate the other more fully, as you are more comfortable and at ease with each other — kissing is permitted, then lay cuddling before going to sleep.

The next morning, bathe together; followed by breakfast, then return to bed.

This time, as you caress and touch, touch and caress the breasts and genitals, making it fun if possible, explore each other with the hands more fully, kiss deeply, building up to sexual intercourse.

Sexual intercourse or penis penetration is a form of sexual massage, arousal, and satisfaction for the partner, receiving this from each other, and not for oneself.

In Tantra the woman puts the penis in her vagina, not the man, to avoid rape or force, and as agreement to penetration by the woman.

The man should practice injaculation (attempting to pull the semen inwards) in order to maintain his erection and sexual intercourse for as long as his partner desires.

Nothing should be done unless agreed by both, but nothing should be avoided through embarrassment — be open with each other about what you like, your sexual fantasies, or, if you are inexperienced and do not know, say so, but also tell your partner, which touches and caresses you like at the moment.

The next day should be spent as was the first day.

The first three days are intended as a 'get to know you as a person, not as a sex object.'

You have now had sex, so any nervousness about that has gone.

You feel more relaxed and at ease with your partner.

You both appreciate and respect, and, hopefully, sexually desire each other.

For the next two days the idea is to raise each other's sexual energy as high as possible.

Use massage, with aromatic oils, incense, and soft music if possible.

Be free, say anything erotic that excites you about your partner, and things you feel will sexually excite him or her.

Be wild, passionate, gentle, romantic, in turn.

Once again, everything that is done must be done with agreement by both — because one partner likes a particular thing does not mean it should be done if the other does not.

You are there to please and excite your partner, and receive the same by giving, not to please only yourself.

For the next three days, there should be a 'plan' to direct the sexual energies to bring about some need in the partner — in physical healing, some material benefit, or spiritual growth.

Doing this for your partner, or, together for someone else, will also have a transforming effect one each other — you may fall in love, or experience visions, or lose fears and anxieties.

Sexual energy is the most effective healing process there is, and the fastest method of spiritual growth, reducing the time from many years, or even many life-times, to a matter of months.

It can help you drop awareness from the mind to the heart, without effort.

An extra day, nine in all, should be added to review what has been experienced by both, and any benefits, and to plan further sessions.

❑❑❑